J. DAWSON

**National Wildlife Federation**

Library of Congress CIP Data: page 95

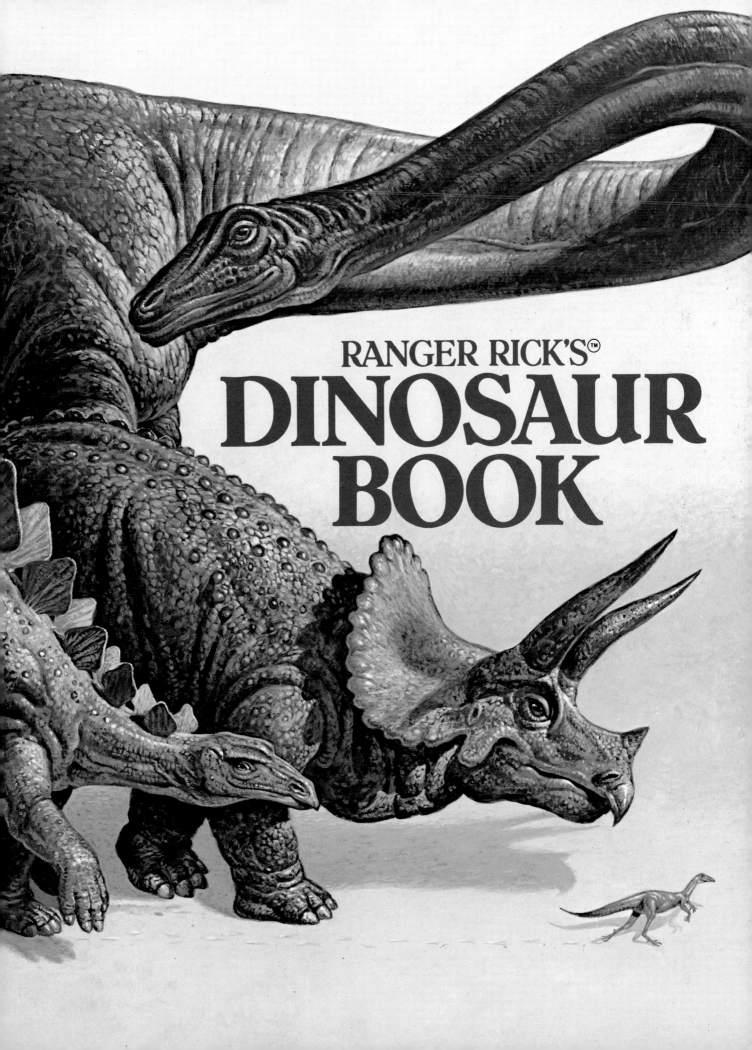

# RANGER RICK'S™
# DINOSAUR BOOK

# Table of Contents

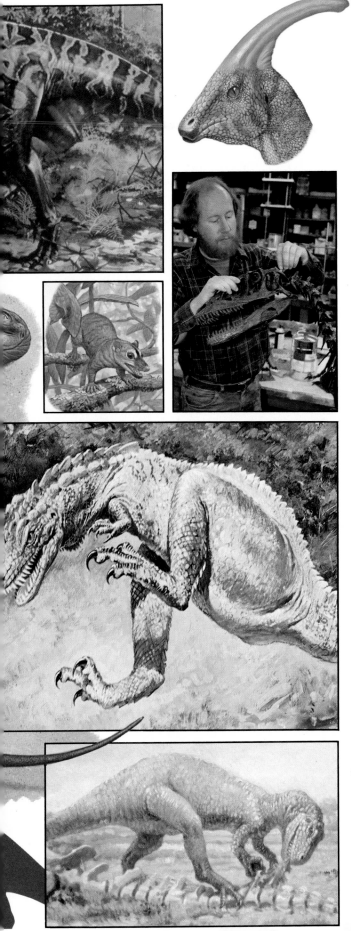

# INTRODUCTION to DINOSAURS

# A Trip in Time

Imagine traveling in a machine that takes you backwards through time. You could visit the Roman Empire or watch the Egyptians build the pyramids. You could even follow cave men hunting for food. But if you went back far enough, you wouldn't see any people at all. In fact, you probably wouldn't see anything that you recognized.

The world you have traveled to is a fantastic place. Continents like Europe and Africa don't exist. All the land in the world forms one huge island, and there is only one ocean. There are no flowering plants, not even dogs or cats. But strange animals roam everywhere.

Where are you? You have gone back millions of years to the *Age of Dinosaurs*. On your time-machine safari you might spot a long-necked giant, twice as tall as a giraffe, nibbling the leaves of a tree. Or an armored monster the size of a car might rumble past you, swinging its heavy tail like a club.

Discovering the Age of Dinosaurs is a grand adventure, and *Ranger Rick's Dinosaur Book* is your personal guide.

# Secrets in Stone

**Q**uestion: What was George Washington's favorite dinosaur?

*Answer:* He didn't have one. Nor did anyone else. No one knew about dinosaurs when Washington was alive. He died in 1799, which was more than 40 years before the word *dinosaur* was first used.

The story of dinosaurs begins in England early in the nineteenth century. Dr. Gideon Mantell and his wife hunted for fossils in their spare time. They enjoyed digging in rock quarries and in cliffs along the coast. There they found the fossils of many fascinating prehistoric plants and animals. Fossil hunters had already dug up bones from ancient giant mammals and sea creatures, but those animals were not dinosaurs.

In the spring of 1822, Mrs. Mantell found a kind of fossil teeth that no one had ever seen. They were shaped like a plant eater's teeth, but they were in rocks much older than those in which fossils of plant eaters had been found.

What could the animal have been? Dr. Mantell sent the teeth and some other bones to the best fossil expert of the day—Baron Cuvier (koo-vee-AY), of Paris, France. Baron Cuvier wrote back that the fossils came from ancient mammals. He said the teeth came from a rhinoceros and the bones came from a hippopotamus.

Dr. Mantell believed that Baron Cuvier was wrong. To him, the teeth didn't look like mammal teeth. He searched in museums until he found an animal whose teeth really looked like the fossil ones. What he found was not a mammal but a lizard—an iguana. He named the creature he found *Iguanodon*. That means "iguana-tooth" in scientific language.

Over the next few years, fossil hunters found the bones of more ancient lizards. Finally, Dr. Richard Owen, a teacher at a college in London, put all the facts together. In 1841, he gave a report to an important group of British

**Iguanodon
(ih-GWON-uh-don)**

scientists. He told them about Iguanodon and the other fossil lizards. He said that they were larger than any lizard ever known. Also, they had stumpy toes and legs like elephants' legs. These animals were so different from other fossil creatures that he put them in a group all to themselves. Then he named the group *Dinosauria*, which means "terrible lizards."

# The Making of a Fossil

The bones, teeth, and claws of animals and parts of plants that have turned into rocks are *fossils*. Many kinds of animal fossils are made this way: An animal that dies in or near water is covered by mud and sand (1). Its flesh decays (2). Over millions of years, more layers of mud and sand pile up. The pressure from the weight of the top layers turns the bottom layers into rock (3).

During all that time, minerals fill up the tiny holes in the bones. Sometimes the bones disintegrate and leave only the minerals, which have taken their shape. The bones are now fossils. Sometimes the rocks are pushed up by an earthquake or rising mountains. Then wind and rain wash the soil and rock away from the fossils (4).

# Dinner in a Dinosaur

Lots of people were excited by the discovery of dinosaurs. An English sculptor named Waterhouse Hawkins built life-sized models of some of them for people to see. His first model was of Iguanodon. When it was nearly finished, he held a banquet for more than a dozen people *inside* the model (right) on New Year's Eve, 1853. The guests included the people who discovered and named Iguanodon. That model and several others are now in Sydenham Park in London (below).

Years later, scientists learned that the shape of the Iguanodon model was wrong. Hawkins had guessed what Iguanodon looked like by studying the few bones that had been found. When whole skeletons were dug up, scientists saw that the creature walked on its hind legs (see pages 8-9) instead of on all four legs. The spike that Hawkins had put on Iguanodon's nose was really one of the animal's thumbs!

# Fossil Hunters

The race to find more fossils of dinosaurs began in England and Europe, but it soon caught on in America. Othniel Charles Marsh and Edward Drinker Cope were America's most famous fossil hunters. These adventurous men showed the world the large number of different kinds of dinosaurs that had lived throughout the American West.

Both Marsh and Cope were expert *paleontologists* (pay-lee-un-TAHL-uh-gists), scientists who learn about the past by finding and identifying fossils. Marsh worked for Yale College in New Haven, Connecticut. At first, Cope didn't work for a university or a museum. He used his own money to pay for his expeditions and had the bones his crews dug up sent by train to his home in Philadelphia, Pennsylvania.

Marsh and Cope were friends at first, but they became strong rivals. In 1869, Marsh told lots of people that Cope had put the neck of a dinosaur skeleton on backwards. A feud began.

When the two men had crews digging for bones in the West, they often spied on each other. Once, Cope sent a telegram about a discovery to newspapers back East. But Marsh had bribed the telegraph operator to give him copies of Cope's messages. When he read of the discovery, Marsh sent out his own story. In it he listed all the mistakes he thought Cope had made in *his* article.

**Othniel Charles Marsh**          **Edward Drinker Cope**

*Fossil hunters in the West had to be ready to fight. Sometimes bandits tried to rob them. And sometimes they traveled where Indians were at war. Professor Marsh (center of back row) and each of his students carried a knife, a revolver, and a rifle in addition to a geologist's tools.*

Cope liked to pull tricks, too. When Marsh's crew started digging at a site in Wyoming, a stranger stopped by to sell them food. After a while, the salesman started asking questions about the bones Marsh's crew was finding. As you might have guessed, the stranger was a spy whom Cope had sent over from his camp.

One time, the men on Marsh's crew really got even. They knew Cope had been spying on them with a telescope. To fool him, they buried a fake skull made up of parts from several different animals. When they knew Cope was watching, they pretended to discover the skull. Cope fell for the trick. When no one was around, he sneaked over to look at the skull. He then wrote an article about what he thought was a new creature.

By working so hard to outdo each other, both Cope and Marsh added greatly to our knowledge of dinosaurs. When the two began their work, only nine North American dinosaurs had been named. Between them, these men discovered and named 136 more.

*These skeletons of adult hadrosaurs are at the American Museum of Natural History in New York City. The one on the left was found by Cope over 100 years ago.*

1. Tyrannosaurus (tie-RAN-uh-saw-rus)
2. Ankylosaurus (an-KYLE-uh-saw-rus)
3. Rhamphorhynchus (ram-for-INK-us)
4. Alioramus (ah-lee-uh-RAH-mus)
5. Struthiomimus (strooth-ee-uh-MY-mus)
6. Parasaurolophus (pair-uh-saw-ROE-luh-fuss)
7. Brachiosaurus (BRACK-ee-uh-saw-rus)
8. Rutiodon (RUE-tee-uh-don)
9. Leptoceratops (lep-toe-SEHR-uh-tops)

# How Big Were They?

**C**an you imagine standing next to a creature tall enough to peek over the top of a two-story house? Or so long it wouldn't fit in the parking space for a school bus? Some dinosaurs were even bigger than that.

Not all dinosaurs were giants, of course. One dinosaur, *Compsognathus* (komp-suh-NAY-thus), was about the size of a chicken. Some were the size of big dogs. But more than half weighed at least as much as a large car, about 4,400 pounds.

The longest complete dinosaur skeleton found so far is from a *Diplodocus* (duh-PLOD-uh-kus). It is 90 feet long. It would reach from home plate to first base on a baseball field. The heaviest dinosaur was *Brachiosaurus* (BRACK-ee-uh-saw-rus). It weighed about 80 tons, as much as ten elephants.

People are still looking for enough bones to put together the greatest giants of them all, nicknamed *Supersaurus* and *Ultrasaurus*. So far, only a few bones have turned up. These giants may have been more than 50 feet tall and 90 feet long. They weighed even more than 80 tons.

Supersaurus and Ultrasaurus were real giants, but they were not the biggest animals of all time. That honor belongs to the blue whale. The largest ones are more than 100 feet long and weigh more than 135 tons.

4 feet

# What Color Were They?

**W**ere dinosaurs gray like elephants, or green like alligators? Or were some colorful, like the red-white-and-blue Arizona coral snake? Could some even change colors as chameleons do? No one knows for sure.

Scientists study fossils to learn what dinosaurs looked like. Most fossils are bones and teeth, the hard parts of an animal's body. Soft

parts with color, like skin, decayed and became part of the soil.

Sometimes scientists find another kind of fossil, called a *cast*. Casts were made when a dinosaur's skin pushed against sand or mud and left a mark. But casts show only where the skin was smooth or bumpy, ridged or scaly. They do not show the skin's color.

Suppose you had never seen a zebra or a photograph of one. Could you tell what one looked like by studying its bones and a cast of its skin? You could see that it was short-haired and shaped like a horse. But you would not know that it had black-and-white stripes.

The only thing to do is to guess what colors the dinosaurs were. Scientists base their guesses on what they know about animals today. They look at where different animals live and at their ways of life. They try to match them with dinosaurs that were about the same size, lived in the same type of habitat, and ate similar kinds of food.

The earliest dinosaurs evolved from animals that looked like crocodiles. Maybe those dinosaurs had the same color patterns that modern crocodiles have: light yellow on their bellies, with patches of black, brown, green, and yellow on their sides and backs.

Some dinosaurs hunted prey the same way leopards (which have spots) and tigers (which have stripes) do. Maybe the dinosaurs had spots or stripes, too.

Plant eaters, like the *Hypacrosaurus* (high-PAK-ruh-saw-rus) at left, spent a lot of time among plants. Skin with patterns of green and black would have blended with the plants and shadows. That would have hidden these gentle beasts from their meat-eating enemies.

The biggest dinosaurs, though, had little need for camouflage. Because they were so large they had few enemies. Like elephants and rhinos, those giants of the past might have been a dull color like gray or brown.

Hypacrosaurus
(high-PAK-ruh-saw-rus)

# Leaping Lizards

Could the two dinosaurs to the right fight on a cold day? Maybe, and maybe not. If they were coldblooded, like reptiles today, they probably couldn't. If they were warm-blooded, like modern mammals, they probably could. If we can learn if dinosaurs were cold-blooded or warmblooded, we will know better what their lives were like.

Modern animals that are coldblooded do not make enough heat inside their bodies to stay warm and active in cold weather. When the air is cold, their bodies are cold and stiff. When the air is warm, their bodies are warm, too, and their muscles work well. As a result, they have energy to chase prey or run away from enemies only when the weather is warm.

Warmblooded animals, such as birds and mammals, make plenty of body heat all the time. This usually lets them stay active even when the weather is cold.

We know that some dinosaurs lived in cold lands. Dinosaur fossils have been found in places that were very cold for part of the year. Large coldblooded animals alive today, such as alligators, can't live where the temperature becomes chilly. How did these dinosaurs survive the cold? Some people think that they were coldblooded and had to migrate to warm places when winter came. Other people think that because these dinosaurs lived in cold lands, they must have been warmblooded.

Other clues about whether or not dinosaurs were cold- or warmblooded are found in their bones. When their bones are put together, they show that dinosaurs stood with their legs straight underneath their bodies. That is the way horses and birds stand. Coldblooded animals, like lizards and crocodiles, stand with their legs sticking out from their sides. They look as if they are doing push-ups, though they aren't. To some scientists, the position of

the dinosaurs' legs is a clue that they might have been warmblooded and very active.

The *inside* of dinosaur bones gives us yet another clue about dinosaurs' bodies. Bones of modern mammals have lots of small tunnels, called *canals*, inside them. Tiny blood vessels are inside the canals. Bones of most kinds of reptiles have very few canals. But the bones of

dinosaurs are like those of mammals. They have many canals.

So far, we don't know for sure what the dinosaurs were really like. Maybe some of them were warmblooded and others were coldblooded. Scientists are looking for more clues to this puzzle and are trying to figure out what the clues mean.

**Dryptosaurus**
**(DRIP-tuh-saw-rus)**

## Bird Hips, Lizard Hips

Dinosaurs were tall and short, skinny and fat. Some had sharp teeth, others had dull ones. But no matter how different they looked, all dinosaurs fit into one of two groups. The members of one group had hip-bones shaped like the hips of lizards (1). Those dinosaurs are called "lizard-hipped," or *saurischian* (saw-RISS-key-un). The members of the other group had hipbones shaped as they are in birds (2). Those dinosaurs are called "bird-hipped," or *ornithischian* (or-ni-THISS-key-un). Scientists no longer use the name *dinosaur* as a scientific term. Instead, they talk about saurischians and ornithischians. But if you tell scientists you want to know about dinosaurs, they still know exactly what animals you mean.

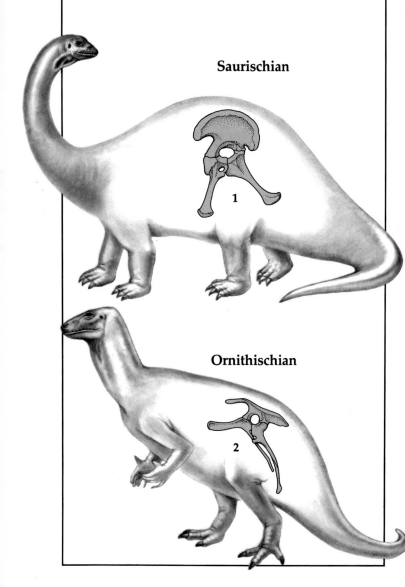

**Saurischian**

1

**Ornithischian**

2

# The Family Tree

The dinosaur family tree to the right covers millions of years. It shows how scientists believe whole families of dinosaurs were related to each other. It also shows approximately when different families of dinosaurs lived and when they became extinct.

The dinosaur family tree starts with reptiles called *cotylosaurs* (coe-TIE-luh-sahrs). These animals, which looked a lot like lizards, lived before the Age of Dinosaurs began. Gradually, over thousands of generations, some of them evolved into mammals. Other members of the cotylosaur family evolved into snakes, lizards, turtles, and other reptiles.

By the time the Age of Dinosaurs began, some cotylosaurs had evolved into yet another new group of animals. These animals were called *thecodonts* (THEE-kuh-dahnts), which means "socket-toothed." Their teeth grew in sockets in their jaws. A part of the thecodont family became crocodiles. Some thecodonts developed into flying reptiles called *pterosaurs* (TAIR-uh-sahrs). Others became the different kinds of dinosaurs.

The gold lines on this family tree connect animal families with their ancestors. Where a family's ancestors are not known for sure, the lines point to where many scientists believe the creatures probably came from.

The Age of Dinosaurs is divided into three very long periods of time. They are shown by the colored areas of the family tree. Dinosaurs appeared in the first period, the *Triassic* (try-ASS-ik). It began about 225 million years ago. The largest dinosaurs lived during the second period, the *Jurassic* (juh-RASS-ik). The last dinosaurs died toward the end of the *Cretaceous* (cree-TAY-shus) period, about 65 million years ago. Altogether, the Age of Dinosaurs lasted about 160 million years. No one knows why dinosaurs became extinct.

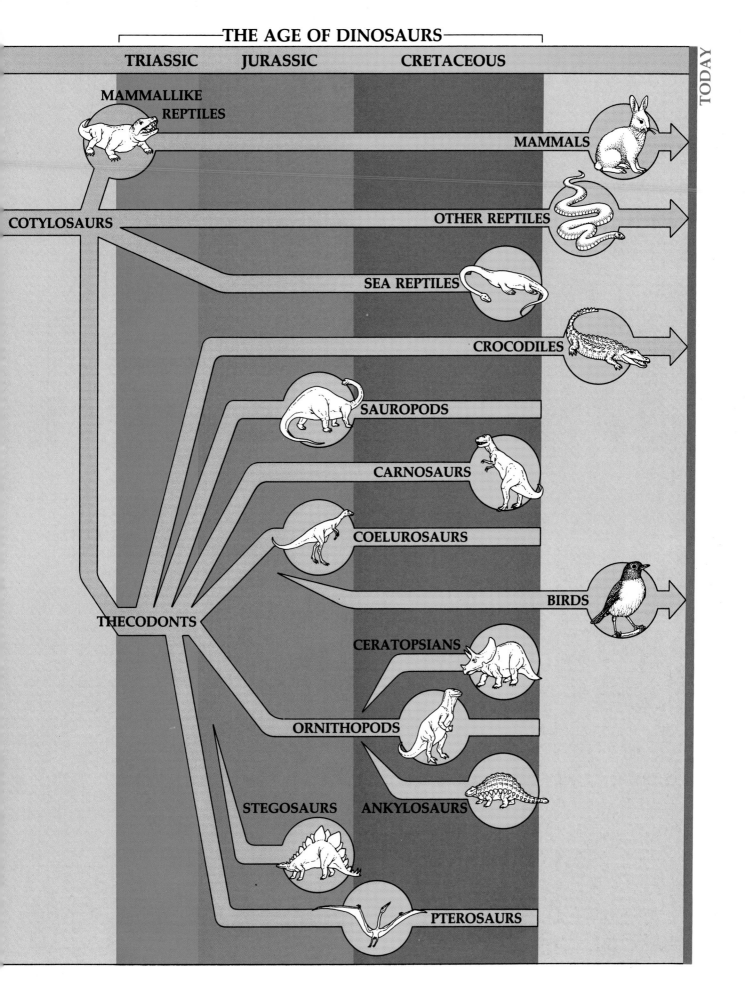

## THE AGE OF DINOSAURS

TRIASSIC    JURASSIC    CRETACEOUS

TODAY

MAMMALLIKE REPTILES

MAMMALS

COTYLOSAURS

OTHER REPTILES

SEA REPTILES

CROCODILES

SAUROPODS

CARNOSAURS

COELUROSAURS

BIRDS

THECODONTS

CERATOPSIANS

ORNITHOPODS

ANKYLOSAURS

STEGOSAURS

PTEROSAURS

# DAWN of the DINOSAURS

Euparkeria
(you-park-AIR-ee-uh)

Cynognathus
(sin-uh-NAY-thus)

# The Rivals

Most people in the United States are used to seasons. Every year has a spring, summer, fall, and winter. But it hasn't always been that way. Millions of years ago, in a period called the *Triassic* (see pages 20-21), there were no seasons. All year long the weather was warm and dry, all over the world.

Other things were different, too. Because it was so dry, large deserts dotted the land. Ferns grew as tall as trees. Plants called *cycads* sprouted up. They had cones and were about as tall as small palm trees. But no grasses or other flowering plants covered the earth. And the earth itself was different. The continents, like North America, Africa, and Europe, didn't exist. All the land in the world was part of one huge "island" called *Pangaea* (pan-JEE-uh).

There were no dinosaurs yet, but their ancestors lived in this strange land. One of them was *Euparkeria* (you-park-AIR-ee-uh). It was a fast and fierce meat-eating animal about the size of a collie dog. On its back were strong scales that protected it.

Imagine what it might have been like one evening in that long-ago place. As the sun sets and the air cools, a hungry Euparkeria takes off across the gullies. It races toward a small water hole that is not far away. Many different animals go there to drink. Euparkeria knows the hunting will be good.

At the water hole, it hides among the cycads near the water's edge. It doesn't have to wait long before a *Lystrosaurus* (list-row-SAW-rus) comes to drink and to eat plants. The Lystrosaurus is cautious but it doesn't detect its enemy. When the Lystrosaurus gets close to the water, Euparkeria suddenly attacks! In three bounds, it reaches its surprised prey and tears open its tough hide.

But unlucky Euparkeria has no time to enjoy its dinner. The smell of blood soon attracts a dog-faced animal called *Cynognathus* (sin-uh-NAY-thus). This beast is slower than

Lystrosaurus
(list-row-SAW-rus)

J. DAWSON

23

Lystrosaurus
(list-row-SAW-rus)
*Mammallike Reptile*

Mandasuchus
(man-duh-SUE-kus)
*Thecodont*

Euparkeria, but it is nearly twice as large and just as ferocious. And it has large fangs and a powerful tail it can use as weapons.

Cynognathus moves in slowly, snarling to show its fangs. Euparkeria hisses a loud warning, but old dog-face ignores it. Suddenly, Cynognathus rushes forward. Euparkeria snatches one last bite of meat from its kill and swiftly runs away. From a safe distance, it watches as its enemy eats its fill.

Fiercely fought battles like this one between Cynognathus and Euparkeria happened often over millions of years. These beasts were rivals. They competed for food and places to raise their families.

Cynognathus belonged to a group of animals called *mammallike reptiles*. So did the Lystrosaurus that Euparkeria killed. People gave them that name because they were a little bit like modern mammals. Some were plant

eaters and some were meat eaters. Some may have had hair and been warmblooded. And some had the same kinds of teeth that mammals have: incisors and canines for cutting and tearing, and molars for grinding.

Euparkeria belonged to another group of reptiles. It was a thecodont (see pages 20-21). Thecodonts came in all sizes and shapes. Some thecodonts, like small Euparkeria, walked on two legs. Others, like the eight-foot-long *Mandasuchus* (man-duh-SUE-kus), walked on all four feet.

The thecodonts and mammallike reptiles were not the only animals alive in the Triassic. The ancestors of today's snakes, lizards, and turtles were alive then too. Another creature of that time was *Scaphonyx* (skuh-FAHN-ix). It was a *rhynchosaur* (RIN-kuh-sahr).

Rhynchosaurs were large and heavy and had broad skulls with beaks that looked like

**Scaphonyx**
**(skuh-FAHN-ix)**
*Rhynchosaur*

**Morganucodon**
**(mor-guh-NEW-kuh-don)**
*Mammal*

**Heterodontosaurus**
**(het-er-uh-DON-tuh-saw-rus)**
*Dinosaur*

the ones on parrots. They used their beaks and powerful jaw muscles to crack the hard shells of the fruits they ate.

Over the ages, the earth's animals changed in many ways. By the end of the Triassic period, most of the mammallike reptiles and rhynchosaurs had died. Small mammals like *Morganucodon* (mor-guh-NEW-kuh-don) had appeared, but there were not very many of them. They were about the size of mice and probably lived in burrows to hide from all the big meat eaters.

The thecodonts changed the most. For millions of years, all reptiles had walked like Scaphonyx. Their legs were on the sides of their bodies, and their bodies were low to the ground. By the middle of the Triassic, some thecodonts had developed legs that held their bodies higher off the ground. These thecodonts moved like crocodiles. Crocodiles sprawl

close to the ground when walking slowly, but raise themselves up when running.

By the end of the Triassic, some thecodonts had changed even more. Their legs were underneath their bodies. Now they could stand upright and move even faster than before. Their legs could also hold up heavier and stronger bodies (see pages 18-19).

The thecodonts developed so many different sizes and shapes that they became a new type of creature, *dinosaurs*. A turkey-sized plant eater called *Heterodontosaurus* (het-er-uh-DON-tuh-saw-rus) was one of the first dinosaurs.

Why did dinosaurs succeed when so many other animals were becoming extinct? The answer may be the animals' legs. Because the first dinosaurs stood upright, they could run faster and more easily than other animals. That let them catch prey and run away from danger more quickly than their competitors.

# The Meat Eaters

Hungry, the dinosaur at right chases a lizard it wants to eat. The dinosaur is about half as long as a car and is as tall as a dining-room table. Its bones are hollow. And it is thin and doesn't weigh as much as a grown man. That is why it can turn sharply and run fast to catch lizards and other quick creatures.

This dinosaur's name is *Coelophysis* (see-low-FIE-sis). Like many of the early dinosaurs, it was a meat eater. There were big meat eaters and little ones. The big ones are called *carnosaurs* (CAR-nuh-sahrs), or "flesh-eating lizards." The little ones are called *coelurosaurs* (see-LURE-uh-sahrs), or "hollow lizards." They were named that because their bones were hollow. The teeth of all the meat eaters were very sharp and could cut thick skin. Meat eaters were dangerous animals.

Coelophysis was one of the biggest of the hollow lizards. It was discovered in 1881 by Edward Cope, the famous American fossil hunter (see page 12). Since then, its bones have been found in New Mexico and the Connecticut Valley. The places where the skeletons were found had been forests with ponds and streams. They were good hunting grounds.

Large Coelophysis skeletons have been found with smaller ones inside them. Maybe these were mothers carrying their young. Or, maybe these dinosaurs were cannibals.

Meat-eating dinosaurs were dangerous hunters, but they didn't always get their prey. In one place in New Mexico, a lot of bones of Coelophysises were found close together. Scientists believe that these dinosaurs might have traveled in packs like wolves or wild dogs. Maybe a pack had chased an animal into quicksand or thick mud and could not get back out. All the dinosaurs in the pack died. Life in the Age of Dinosaurs was dangerous for *all* the animals.

## Making Tracks

This girl is looking at dinosaur tracks in Dinosaur State Park in Connecticut. The tracks were found in 1966 as the ground was being dug up for a new building. The size and shape of the tracks and the distance between them show that they were left by an early meat eater—probably a "hollow lizard"—about 8 feet tall and 20 feet long.

Scientists have compared the distance between footprints in tracks left by hollow lizards with the distance between footprints in tracks left by living animals. They found that these dinosaurs could run only about 10 miles an hour. That's almost as fast as most 10-year-old children can run.

**Coelophysis**
**(see-low-FIE-sis)**

## The Roadrunner

The roadrunner, which lives in the desert in the American Southwest, is built a lot like a coelurosaur, or "hollow lizard." In fact, some scientists think the roadrunner and all other birds evolved from the coelurosaurs. Like the hollow lizards, the roadrunner has hollow bones that make it lightweight and a long tail that it uses for balance when running. And also like a coelurosaur, the bird is a fast runner. It captures small mammals, insects, lizards, and snakes. This food is the same kind the hollow lizards probably ate.

27

# The Plant Eaters

The story of the early dinosaurs isn't complete without the plant eaters. The first ones looked a little bit like the lightweight meat eaters. Both groups had long necks and small heads. But the plant eaters were much longer and fatter than the meat eaters.

*Plateosaurus* (PLAY-tee-uh-saw-rus), shown here, was one of the largest of the early plant eaters. It grew to be about 26 feet long, longer than a large car.

The name *Plateosaurus* means "flat lizard." Of course, the animal wasn't flat. The name refers to its teeth, which were flat on top rather than pointed. Its flat teeth were good for pulling off leaves, but not for grinding them up into small pieces.

How did the "flat lizards" grind up their food so it could be digested easily? Some scientists think that flat lizards solved the problem by swallowing small rocks. The rocks moved around in a dinosaur's stomach, and the leaves were crushed between the rocks. The reason these scientists believe this is that piles of small, round stones have been found near the bones of some plant-eating dinosaurs. These rocks are called "bellystones."

The use of bellystones is not that strange. Many birds swallow small pebbles which go into organs near their stomachs. The organs are called *gizzards*. There, the pebbles grind up grain and other food. Crocodiles of today also swallow rocks to help grind up food.

But other scientists don't think dinosaurs had bellystones. They say that rocks that look like bellystones are found in places where there aren't any dinosaur bones. And they say that many plant eaters' skeletons are found without bellystones anywhere around. If these dinosaurs *had* to swallow rocks to grind up food, then all their skeletons should have bellystones near them.

Scientists are not sure what happened to this first group of plant-eating dinosaurs. All of the group had died by the end of the Triassic period. But later, a new group of plant eaters would evolve. Some of them would be the largest land animals of all time.

## On the Move

These caribou are migrating to their breeding grounds in northern Canada. Their journey is over 600 miles long. Dinosaurs that ate plants may also have migrated. Skeletons of Plateosaurus have been found in southern Germany in a place that used to be a desert. The desert was between an inland sea and mountains. The dino-saurs lived in the mountains for part of the year. During the dry season, the dinosaurs may have left the mountains and crossed the desert to reach the inland sea. The trip was about 75 miles long and some of the weaker animals died. Their bones were covered by sand. They stayed there, undisturbed, for more than 190 million years.

# Strange Swimmers

Dinosaurs weren't the only animals alive during the Age of Dinosaurs. Dinosaurs did take over the land, but many other kinds of reptiles lived in the rivers and lakes and in the huge ocean.

*Phytosaurs* (FIE-tuh-sahrs) (1) were the most common reptiles that lived in freshwater streams and marshes. They grew to be 15 feet long. Their short legs and powerful tails made them excellent swimmers. They resembled modern crocodiles, but the two creatures are not closely related. One difference is that a crocodile's nose is on the tip of its snout. A phytosaur's nose grew on its forehead. That let the animal breathe while it held on to fish struggling in the water.

At the edge of the sea, *placodonts* (PLACK-uh-dahnts) (2) fed on shellfish and snails. They raked their food off the shallow bottom with their claws and teeth. (Walruses probably use their tusks the same way to dig up food.) Because they had fat bodies and short necks, placodonts looked like giant turtles. And like turtles, they may also have dragged themselves onto the land to lay eggs.

5

Phytosaurs and placodonts walked on land, swam in water, and probably laid eggs. *Ichthyosaurs* (ICK-thee-uh-sahrs) (3) never left the sea, and they didn't lay eggs. They bore live young, just as whales and some sharks do. Full-grown ichthyosaurs measured up to 30 feet long and looked like modern dolphins or swordfish. Their streamlined bodies and powerful tails helped them race through the water after fish and other prey. They even had special bones around their eyes to protect them from the pressure of the water.

If you saw a *nothosaur* (NO-thu-sahr) (4), you probably would think it was a lizard in the sea. Nothosaurs had unusually long necks and tails, but they were still less than half as long as the ichthyosaurs. Paddling around with their webbed feet, they looked for fish. They probably crawled onto shore to rest and mate, just as seals and walruses do today.

Of all the reptiles that lived in the sea, *Tanystropheus* (tan-iss-TROE-fee-us) (5) was the most amazing looking. This creature looked a lot like a lizard except for one thing: Its neck was ten feet long. The neck was almost as long as the rest of the animal! Despite its great length, the neck had only ten bones. That's one less than in a tiny parakeet's neck.

Tanystropheus may have stood on shore and searched the water for food. But, more likely, it stayed in the water and never went ashore. Scientists say that the animal's neck bones didn't have any place that large muscles could have attached to. And without large muscles, Tanystropheus could not raise its heavy neck into the air. The water probably helped hold up the long neck, much as it holds up beach balls.

In the long run, it didn't matter how Tanystropheus used its long neck. All those animals died before the next time period began. So did most of the other reptiles that lived in the water. Only the ichthyosaurs survived. They would be joined later by even larger water creatures, including a 40-foot-long "ribbon reptile" and a 50-foot-long "horror crocodile" (see pages 76-77).

1. **phytosaur (FIE-tuh-sahr)**
2. **placodont (PLACK-uh-dahnt)**
3. **ichthyosaur (ICK-thee-uh-sahr)**
4. **nothosaur (NO-thu-sahr)**
5. **Tanystropheus (tan-iss-TROE-fee-us)**

HaLLett '84

# TIME of the GIANTS

J. DAWSON

# A Herd of Titans

Over 35 million years have passed since the beginning of the Age of Dinosaurs. Many things have changed. The big island of Pangaea has split up into several pieces. South America, Antarctica, Australia, and India have broken away. They have become separate continents. The climate around the world is still mild, but some places now have rainy and dry seasons. Our time machine has taken us to the Jurassic period, the middle part of the Age of Dinosaurs (see pages 20-21).

Most of the mammallike reptiles have died. So have most of the thecodonts. Dinosaurs are now the most important creatures on the land. A few are as small as turkeys, but most are big. This period is famous for its giants. One of these giants was a plant eater known as *Apatosaurus* (ah-PAT-uh-saw-rus). Herds of them roamed what is now the American West. Here is a scene that might have happened.

A herd of apatosaurs has begun to travel across a desert. The rainy season is over and the herd's forest home is dry. If the huge plant eaters don't reach the lake on the other side of the desert, they will die of thirst.

A hungry youngster lags behind and moves away from the herd. It sneaks back to the forest and looks for low-growing plants. This youngster is nearly 15 feet long, but it is too small to reach the tops of the tall pine trees.

As the youngster heads deeper into the dark forest, it eagerly tears leaves and twigs from any plant it can reach. Suddenly, a noise in the woods warns of danger. The scared youngster runs quickly out of the forest and back toward the herd.

It has not gone far into the desert when a half-grown *Allosaurus* (AL-uh-saw-rus) wanders out of the woods. That's what had made the noise. The Allosaurus doesn't know that the young apatosaur is nearby.

The Allosaurus is a terrifying sight. It has long, sharp teeth and claws. Soon it spots the youngster running away and chases after it. The Allosaurus, too, is hungry.

The young apatosaur now runs faster than it has ever run before, all the while looking for its mother. But the Allosaurus is faster. The meat eater catches up with its victim and tries to jump onto its back. But, surprise! The apatosaur's heavy tail swings around and knocks the attacker off its feet.

Safe for a moment, the youngster races on. But the Allosaurus soon gets up, and the chase is on again. Blind to all but its escaping dinner, the Allosaurus fails to sense its own danger. Suddenly, the meat eater finds itself facing a dozen angry parents. They have come to save the frightened youngster. Now it is the Allosaurus's turn to run away. It is no match for the 30-ton, 75-foot-long giants. At last, the young apatosaur is safe.

The frightened young apatosaur and its herd were members of the *sauropod* (SAW-ruh-pod) group of plant-eating dinosaurs. Herds of

**Apatosaurus**
**(ah-PAT-uh-saw-rus)**

# Moving On

Sauropods had at least two things in common with elephants: First, they were very large plant eaters. Second, they traveled in herds. Dinosaur footprints uncovered in Texas show the tracks of many sauropods traveling together in herds. The Texas tracks also show that the young dinosaurs traveled at the center of the herd. There they were protected by the adults. That is the way many elephant herds travel.

Herds of elephants may number 10 to 50 animals. The size of sauropod herds is not known for certain, but scientists have found evidence of a group of 19 moving together in the same direction.

Some scientists also think that sauropods lived in the same kind of habitat that elephants live in: the plains and forests of a hot, dry land.

sauropods probably wandered over most of the world. We think this because their fossils have been found on nearly every continent, from the Americas to Asia and Australia.

In a period famous for having many giant dinosaurs, the sauropods were the tallest, the heaviest, and the longest of them all.

The longest dinosaur that ever lived was *Diplodocus* (duh-PLOD-uh-kus). It measured 90 feet from nose to tail. (See the drawing on page 38.) Though Diplodocus was long, it was lighter than many of the other sauropods. Still, it weighed more than two elephants.

The most famous members of the sauropod family were the apatosaurs. For a long time, the bulky apatosaur was called *Brontosaurus* (BRON-tuh-saw-rus). That popular name means "thunder lizard." It describes the thundering noise these giants might have made when traveling.

Later, scientists realized that the same creature had already been named *Apatosaurus*. Under the rules that scientists follow, the first name used is the one that must be kept. So, the name *Brontosaurus* was dropped.

Thunder lizards have changed more than their names. They have also changed their heads! When the first Apatosaurus fossils were dug up in 1877, no skulls were found. Later, a skull was dug up near where several skeletons had been found. Scientists put that skull on an Apatosaurus skeleton on display in a museum.

In 1909, another skull was found even closer to where Apatosaurus bones were found. This skull was longer and flatter than the other one. After many years of study, scientists finally agreed that the old skull belonged to a different kind of dinosaur. At a ceremony in 1978, the original skull on the skeleton in the museum was replaced with the new one.

## Messages in the Mud

In the 1930's, scientists in Texas found some unusual tracks. They were sauropod tracks, but there was no track of the animal's tail dragging the ground as there was in another place nearby. Why not? Some scientists say the sauropod was running in shallow water, and its tail was floating. They think the water was shallow because the footprints are deep. If the dinosaur had been in deeper water, it would have floated more and left shallower footprints.

There was another surprise, too. The men found tracks of a three-toed creature, a meat eater, following the sauropod. Did the predator catch its prey? The answer is still hidden beneath a hill.

Other ideas about the sauropods have changed, too. Scientists once thought that these dinosaurs were so heavy they couldn't walk on land. Their legs couldn't have held them up unless they lived in water up to their necks. In water, their huge bodies would have acted like floating balloons and taken some of the weight off their legs.

Now some scientists say the sauropods lived mostly on dry land. What proof do they have? First, these dinosaurs' bones have been found with fossils of plants and animals that lived on land. Second, sauropods look more like modern elephants, which live on land, than like animals such as crocodiles, which live in shallow water. Third, scientists decided that if a sauropod waded up to its neck in water, it could not have breathed. The pressure of the water on its chest would have kept its lungs from inflating.

# Biggest of the Big

Brachiosaurus (BRACK-ee-uh-saw-rus)

The heaviest and tallest sauropods were the *brachiosaurs* (BRACK-ee-uh-sahrs), or "arm lizards." Unlike other sauropods, the brachiosaurs had front legs that were longer than their back ones. The long front legs raised the creatures' necks and heads higher than all the other animals around.

There were at least five kinds of brachiosaurs. The largest member of the group was called *Brachiosaurus.* It towered 40 feet high and weighed 80 tons. That is more than twice as tall as a giraffe and as heavy as ten large African elephants.

A complete brachiosaur skeleton is on exhibit in a museum in Berlin, East Germany. It is the largest dinosaur skeleton on display anywhere in the world. During World War II, much of the city was destroyed—but somehow the skeleton survived.

Brachiosaurus may someday have to take second or third place behind even bigger dinosaurs. In the 1970's, scientists found a few bones that look as if they came from two super-sized brachiosaurs. A single neck bone of one of these creatures was nearly as long as a grown person. A whole skeleton has not been found yet. But if one is, scientists say it might reach 50 feet high. The whole animal probably weighed nearly 100 tons.

These new creatures have not been named. So far, they just have nicknames: "Supersaurus" and "Ultrasaurus."

Scientists wonder how those giants could get enough to eat. A large elephant may have to eat for 16 to 18 hours a day to supply its body with energy. What did a brachiosaur do if it had to eat several times as much food as an elephant? One idea is that it didn't have to eat that much. Maybe it was coldblooded and slow moving instead of warmblooded and active. That way it could get by on much less food because it needed less energy.

Another puzzle about the brachiosaur is its nose. The openings for the nose are near the top of the animal's skull. Elephant skulls are built the same way, but elephants breathe through long trunks. Did brachiosaurs have trunks, too? So far, no one knows.

## The Lookouts

Giraffes and brachiosaurs may have a lot in common. Like brachiosaurs, giraffes have extra-long necks. They also have front legs that are longer than their back ones. Giraffes are the tallest animals alive today, just as brachiosaurs were the tallest during the Age of Dinosaurs. Because of their height, giraffes can eat leaves in the tops of trees. So could brachiosaurs. And giraffes make good lookouts. Smaller animals, like zebras, graze nearby until the giraffes spot danger. Then the giraffes and the zebras run to safety. Because brachiosaurs were so tall, they may also have been good lookouts.

**1. Mussaurus (moose-SAW-rus)**

**2. Ultrasaurus leg bones**

**3. Diplodocus (duh-PLOD-uh-kus)**

**4. Apatosaurus (ah-PAT-uh-saw-rus)**

# From Small to Tall

The smallest and the largest dinosaur skeletons ever found came from the prosauropods and the sauropods.

The smallest dinosaur skeleton was a baby prosauropod named *Mussaurus* (moose-SAW-rus), the "mouse reptile" (no. 1). Dr. José Bonaparte found it in Argentina in 1977. Only eight inches long, the mouse reptile easily fits in a human's hands. When grown up, Mussaurus would have been about 20 feet long.

Scientist James Jensen looks tiny next to the leg bones of the sauropod *Ultrasaurus* (no. 2). He discovered these bones in Colorado in 1979. A complete creature (no. 6) would have been around 50 feet tall. That is nearly three times as tall as a giraffe. If it were that tall, Ultrasaurus would be the tallest dinosaur ever found. Dr. Jensen also discovered *Supersaurus*, probably the second tallest dinosaur (no. 5). He found it in 1972.

The longest complete dinosaur skeleton came from a Diplodocus (no. 3). It is 90 feet long. Apatosaurus, once called Brontosaurus, is probably the most famous of the giant dinosaurs. It was about 75 feet long and weighed about 30 tons (no. 4).

How long did it take the giants to grow so big? No one knows for sure. Some scientists believe that dinosaurs, like modern reptiles, grew all their lives. That may have been for 100, possibly even 200 years—or longer!

5. Supersaurus

6. Ultrasaurus

# The Plated Lizards

Among the oddest-looking dinosaurs of all were the *stegosaurs* (STEG-uh-sahrs), or "plated lizards" (below, right).

Large, diamond-shaped plates made two rows down the center of the creature's back. The rows even went up its neck and down its tail. The plates were made of bone. Each one was about two inches thick and was probably covered with tough, bumpy skin. The largest plates were two feet wide and two feet high.

Scientists are not sure why *Stegosaurus* had these plates. They wonder if the plates stood up all the time or lay flat when not in use. They also wonder if the plates were brightly colored. Colors could have attracted mates or warned other stegosaurs to stay away. The plates may have made Stegosaurus look larger. That could have helped scare off its enemies.

The plates might also have served as radiators. Marks on the plates show that large blood vessels were next to the bone. Sunlight hitting the plates would have heated the blood

**Ceratosaurus**
**(sehr-AT-uh-saw-rus)**

40

inside the vessels. That could have kept Stegosaurus warm on a cool day. At other times, wind blowing around the plates would have cooled the blood. That could have kept the dinosaur from overheating on a hot day.

Stegosaurus's tail was also weird. It was about half as long as a car. Four sharp spikes, each nearly three feet long, stuck out near its tip. Whenever Stegosaurus walked, the tail swung back and forth.

Part of what makes Stegosaurus so odd-looking is its shape. Its back legs were eleven feet high, but its front legs were only about four feet high. That meant that Stegosaurus's rear end stuck way up in the air. At the same time, its beak was down close to the ground, where it nibbled soft plants.

The dinosaur's head looked too small for its body, too. Although Stegosaurus was 25 feet long and weighed 4,000 pounds, its head was only 16 inches long. Its brain was the size of a golf ball and weighed two ounces. That's how much one half a stick of butter weighs.

Such a tiny brain needed help to manage such a large body. A thick clump of nerves near the two biggest plates helped control the hind legs and the spiked tail. Some scientists think that this clump of nerves was larger than the animal's brain. In fact, they say Stegosaurus had two brains.

Other scientists say the second "brain," or clump of nerves, was probably smaller than the real brain. They looked at the opening in the backbone where the nerves were clumped together. Then they compared it with a similar opening in the backbones of birds. That area also holds clumps of nerves. But it holds something else, too: a chemical called *glycogen*. Birds use glycogen to store food energy until they need it. Maybe Stegosaurus stored glycogen, too. When an enemy attacked, the dinosaur could have used its glycogen for extra energy to fight or run away.

Stegosaurus
(STEG-uh-saw-rus)

# Heavy Hunters

The largest meat eaters during the Jurassic period were the carnosaurs. They must have been successful hunters. Their fossils have been found in North America, Europe, China, India, and even Australia.

*Allosaurus* (AL-uh-saw-rus), the largest of the carnosaurs, was 36 feet long. It weighed over 4,000 pounds, more than a big car.

Usually, Allosaurus hunted creatures smaller than itself. But at times it ate larger dinosaurs. The skeleton of one huge sauropod shows toothmarks where an allosaur bit into the plant eater's tail bone.

Those tooth marks raise a big question, though. Did the hungry allosaur really chase and catch the giant plant eater? Allosaurus's legs were built for running fast. The slower plant eater probably could not outrun it.

But if the allosaur did catch and kill the plant eater, why did it bother chewing on the bony tail? After all, there would have been plenty of good meat farther up on the body.

Most likely the big dinosaur was already dead when the allosaur found it. At least that's what many scientists think. They say that Allosaurus was a scavenger. Scavengers are animals that live off the remains of other animals that died or were killed. But Allosaurus may have been an active hunter part of the time, too. It could have killed some animals to eat and also fed on the remains of others, the way hyenas do.

Allosaurus was only one of many different kinds of carnosaurs. Some carnosaurs appear to have been able to swim after prey that tried escaping across deep water. Tracks of just the tips of a carnosaur's toes have been found. These tracks suggest that the animals were swimming by pushing themselves off the bottom of a lake or river with their feet.

A few tracks suggest that some carnosaurs

traveled in groups. Maybe they hunted in packs the way wolves, hyenas, and wild dogs do. Once they had eaten all they wanted and left, Allosaurus and other scavengers would eat the rest of the remains.

No matter how Allosaurus got its food, it was well designed for eating. Its lower jaw could drop even lower than usual if it had to.

**Ornitholestes chasing Archaeopteryx**

# The Ancient Wing

**Archaeopteryx**
**(are-key-OP-ter-ix)**

**W**orkers in a German quarry in 1861 uncovered a puzzle that has not been solved after more than 120 years. The puzzle was a new fossil that had a wishbone like a bird's and wings with feathers. It was a bird, the earliest ever found. It was named *Archaeopteryx* (are-key-OP-ter-ix), the "ancient wing."

One of the puzzling things about this bird was its ancestors. To try to solve this puzzle, scientists checked its head, its tail, its hands, its feet. Finally, one man studied the fossil for two years and listed 21 ways that its bones matched those of the small, meat-eating dinosaurs called coelurosaurs (see pages 44-45).

Archaeopteryx was a very primitive bird. It has been called a missing link in the evolutionary chain between the dinosaurs and modern birds. In some ways it was like a dinosaur. In other ways it was like a bird. It had teeth and a bony tail like a dinosaur. Birds today don't have teeth, and their tails are just long feathers. But, like birds, Archaeopteryx had wings and feathers.

Scientists still don't know for sure why this ancient bird had feathers or whether or not it could fly. Feathers help birds in many ways. Of course, they help birds fly. They also insulate them and help them stay warm. Perhaps feathers began as insulators. Small, warmblooded dinosaurs would have lost heat very quickly. Feathers would have helped keep their bodies at a constant temperature.

The feathers might have served other uses. Some people think that Archaeopteryx ran along the ground, chasing insects and other small prey. When it got close enough, it used its wide, feathered wings to scoop up its meal.

Archaeopteryx probably could not fly, at least the way most birds do today. It did not have the right bones for holding the muscles needed to flap its wings.

But Archaeopteryx might have been able to glide. That's what flying squirrels do. Some scientists think the bird climbed branches in search of prey, then spread its wings and floated gently back to the ground. Other scientists think it lived only on the ground.

# Flying Dragons

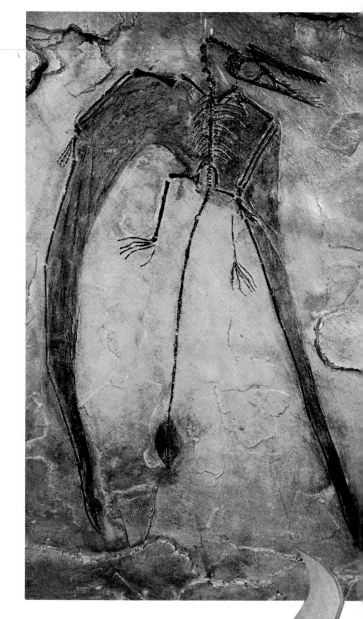

**D**inosaurs ruled the forests and plains of the earth, but other creatures mastered the skies above them. Those flyers were not birds, but reptiles called *pterosaurs* (TAIR-uh-sahrs), the "winged lizards." Among them were the first backboned animals that could fly rather than just glide like a flying squirrel.

Each of a pterosaur's wings stretched from the body to the end of the fourth finger. That finger is visible in the picture of the *Rhamphorhynchus* (ram-for-INK-us) skeleton to the right. The fourth finger was the front edge of the wing. In small flyers, it was a few inches long. In large flyers, it was up to 20 feet long.

The other three fingers were short and had sharp claws. The claws might have helped the pterosaurs catch prey or climb trees.

Some pterosaurs had large shoulder and chest bones. These bones supported the big muscles needed to flap wings. Other pterosaurs probably were gliders rather than flappers. The shape of their wings seems best suited for riding columns of rising warm air.

**Dimorphodon**
**(die-MOHR-fuh-don)**

**Rhamphorhynchus**
**(ram-for-INK-us)**

48

*Dimorphodon* (die-MOHR-fuh-don) was one of the first pterosaurs. Its head looked way too large for its eagle-sized body. It had sharp teeth, claws on its hands and feet, and a skinny tail like a rat's tail.

*Rhamphorhynchus* had a wingspan of four feet but a body barely 18 inches long. Its curved beak had sharp teeth that slanted forward. These teeth might have helped the flyer spear fish when it dived into the water.

Rhamphorhynchus also had a stiff tail. At its end was a small, diamond-shaped flap of skin. The flap probably acted as a rudder to help the creature steer as it flew.

*Pterodactylus* (tair-uh-DAK-till-us) skeletons of many sizes have been found. Some skeletons are as small as sparrows. Others are as large as hawks. The skeletons show that Pterodactylus had a very short tail and thin, delicate teeth. This flying reptile probably ate insects that it caught while it was in the air.

Being able to fly or glide offered many benefits. Pterosaurs could easily escape from most predators. They could raise their families high in trees or on rocky slopes, out of reach of hungry meat eaters. By swooping down out of the sky, they could catch insects or fish better than ever.

Whether they were flappers or gliders, one thing is certain. Pterosaurs were the lords of the air for millions of years before the birds took their place.

## Furry Flaps

Flying squirrels and pterosaurs have a lot in common. A squirrel's wings are flaps of skin that lie along its sides when the squirrel is walking, but stretch out to form wings when the squirrel leaps from a tree. A pterosaur's wings were also flaps of skin stretched between its fingers and its sides. Pterosaurs may have been warmblooded and furry, as flying squirrels are. But there is a big difference: Flying squirrels glide, not fly. Most pterosaurs could beat their wings and fly as modern birds do.

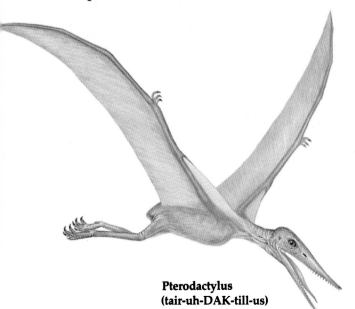

**Pterodactylus
(tair-uh-DAK-till-us)**

# SEASONS of CHANGE

# Creatures with Crests

Our journey through time is more than half over. We have reached the Cretaceous period, the last part of the Age of Dinosaurs. It was also the longest part. It lasted from about 135 million to 65 million years ago. During that time, the continents drifted near to where they are today. But still the world was not like it is now.

A large part of central North America was covered by a shallow sea. Central America was under water. Europe was a large group of islands. Toward the end of this period, new mountain ranges such as the Rockies were beginning to rise.

The earth's climate changed during this time. Instead of steady tropical heat with rainy and dry seasons, the weather grew a little bit cooler. Before the period ended, modern trees such as oaks and hickories appeared. Grass and colorful flowering plants also evolved.

Dinosaurs and other reptiles were still masters of the land, sea, and air. In some places, small mammals and birds had become fairly common. But dinosaurs were still the most important creatures. Many of the old dinosaur families had died out. In their places came many new kinds in even more unusual shapes. More kinds of dinosaurs lived now than had ever lived before.

Among the most widespread dinosaurs were the *hadrosaurs* (HAD-ruh-sahrs). They lived all over the world. These plant eaters had noses like the bills on ducks. In fact, they are called *duck-billed* dinosaurs. Some of them had strangely shaped crests on their heads. And some of them probably traveled in herds.

Try to picture one of those herds on a bright spring day 75 million years ago. Some duck-billed dinosaurs called *corythosaurs* (coe-RITH-uh-sahrs) had finally arrived at their breeding grounds in a place that is now part of western Canada. They had gone there to feed, find mates, and lay their eggs.

A young male *Corythosaurus* had hatched there several years earlier. Now he was old enough to take a mate for himself. It would not be easy. There were few young females. The older ones belonged to harems guarded by the older, bigger males. The harem masters would try to keep all the females.

As he was walking to a stream to drink, the young corythosaur spotted a lone female browsing on the leaves and twigs of the forest plants. He trumpeted by forcing the air in his chest up his throat, through the hollow crest on his head, and out his bill. The air vibrating in the crest made his voice rich and deep.

The female stopped eating and turned in his direction. She answered with a song of her own. As the male approached, she noticed the flame-orange color of his crest and mane. These were signs that he was old enough to mate. The two honked and trumpeted their mating calls back and forth to each other.

The young duckbill had almost reached the female when a large body smashed into him from behind. He fell to the ground. As he got up, he saw that it was an older male corythosaur that had knocked him down. That duckbill also wanted the female for a mate.

Corythosaurus
(coe-RITH-uh-saw-rus)

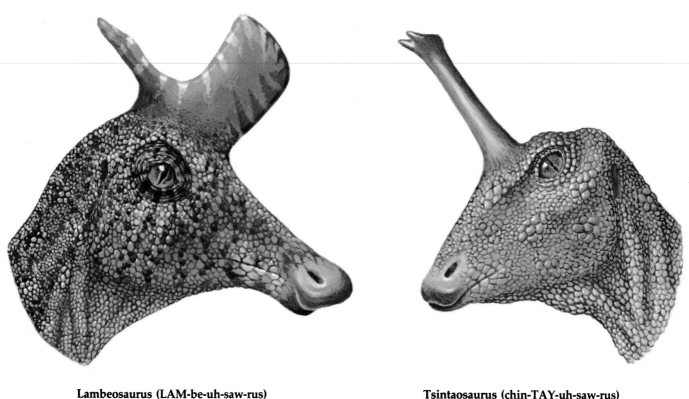

Lambeosaurus (LAM-be-uh-saw-rus)　　　　　Tsintaosaurus (chin-TAY-uh-saw-rus)

The young male lunged at his rival. He shoved the other dinosaur with his shoulder. Then he whacked him with his heavy tail. Honking with rage, the older male tried to bite the younger one, but missed. Thump! The young male's tail struck again. It hit the rival male so hard it knocked him to the ground.

After that, the rival backed away, honking in anger. The younger male answered with a booming call that could be heard above the calls of all the other duckbills in the forest. Then he walked over to the female, and she nuzzled him gently. They moved off together into the forest. He had found a mate.

Fossils tell us a lot about the duck-billed dinosaurs like Corythosaurus. Some of them were 40 feet long and 20 feet high and weighed about 10,000 pounds. Their front legs were short, and they walked upright on their strong back legs. They stretched their long tails out behind them for balance. By measuring the distance between a duckbill's footprints, scientists figured out that these dinosaurs traveled about five miles per hour.

## A Dinosaur's Nest

Nests and eggs help show how hadrosaurs and other dinosaurs lived. The underside of one dinosaur nest (left)—not that of a hadrosaur—shows the bottoms of the eggs unbroken. That means the young probably left the nest right after hatching. If they had stayed, they would have crushed their shells. Nearby, hadrosaur nests were full of broken shells. That means those young stayed in their nests after hatching. The parents probably took care of them.

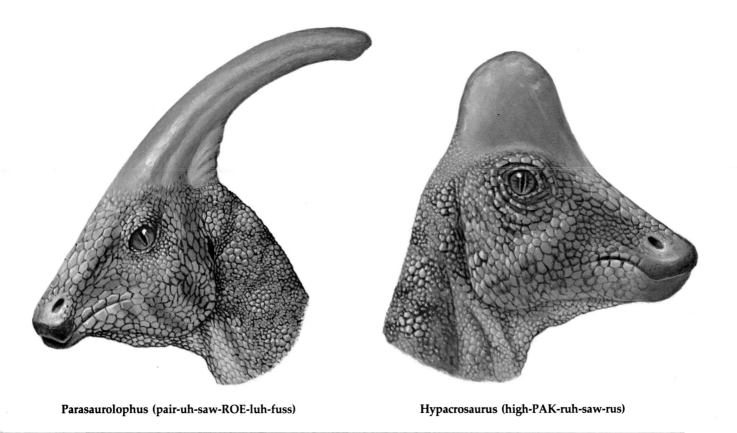

**Parasaurolophus (pair-uh-saw-ROE-luh-fuss)**

**Hypacrosaurus (high-PAK-ruh-saw-rus)**

Scientists once thought that the duck-billed dinosaurs lived in swamps. The animals' duck-like bills, webbed hands, and tails seemed to be designed for living in water. Now scientists think that these dinosaurs lived in forests. Scientists changed their minds when fossilized, undigested food was found in the stomach area of a duckbill. The food included twigs, pine needles, leaves, and seeds. That is the food of land animals, not water dwellers.

Duck-billed dinosaurs had more than 100 teeth to help grind up their food. As old teeth wore out, new ones replaced them.

The most curious part of a duckbill was the unusual crest on its head. These crests were many different shapes and sizes. Four of them are shown above. All of these four types of crests were hollow, but some of the other crests were made of solid bone.

Scientists are not sure what purpose the crests served. It was once thought that the crests were snorkels and that a swimming duckbill breathed by sticking its crest out of the water. But then it was found that there were no openings at the top of the crests. They couldn't have been used as snorkels because there was no way for air to enter them from outside.

Air passages inside the crests did open into the dinosaurs' noses. Perhaps the crests improved the dinosaurs' sense of smell.

Another idea is that the crests helped the animals tell one another apart. During the mating season, the males' crests may have changed color. That happens in birds and many other animals alive today. Brightly colored crests would have attracted mates or warned other males to keep away.

Some duckbills also had "manes." These were folds of skin that ran up their backs all the way from their tails to their necks. A brightly colored mane and crest would have made a really impressive courtship display.

Some duck-billed dinosaurs probably traveled in herds. If the crests made the animals' voices louder or different, that would have helped mates and parents find each other in the herd. When one duckbill called to another, the sound would have bounced around inside the crest and come out louder and richer. A megaphone amplifies a cheerleader's voice in much the same way.

Whatever their use, crests must have served the duckbills well. These dinosaurs were around for millions of years and were very common in most parts of the world.

# Battling Boneheads

As the hadrosaurs spread through the river valleys, another group of dinosaurs moved across the hills and plains. They were the *pachycephalosaurs* (pack-ee-SEF-uh-low-sahrs), the "boneheaded" dinosaurs.

The boneheads were curious-looking plant eaters. They had no tall plates on their bodies or spikes on their tails as the stegosaurs did. They had no long necks and huge bodies as the sauropods did. They did not even have duckbills or mouths with hundreds of teeth like the hadrosaurs.

What they did have were thick domes on top of their heads. Some of the creatures also had spikes and big warts on their faces.

Different bonehead dinosaurs had different kinds of spikes and domes. Some boneheads had spikes that formed rings around their heads. The domes were made of bone that had grown up to ten inches thick. That is thicker than your entire head.

Some boneheads had thick, rounded domes. Others had flatter, thinner domes. Some had domes made of a single piece of thick bone. Others had domes made up of smaller pieces of bone joined together. And some boneheads had domes that were rougher than others. Scientists think that females had the lighter, smoother domes. The heavier, rougher domes might have belonged to males.

Some scientists think these dinosaurs used the spikes on their faces to dig up tasty plants. Others say the boneheads used the spikes to drive off enemies.

What the domes were used for is also a mystery. Maybe the thick skulls were caused by overactive growth glands and had no special purpose at all. Or maybe the dinosaurs used them to push their way through underbrush when they ran away from danger. Such

Pachycephalosaurus
(pack-ee-SEF-uh-low-saw-rus)

54

modern birds as cassowaries and guinea fowl use their extra-thick skulls that way.

One popular idea is that these dinosaurs used their boneheads to butt each other. Males could have fought each other for territory or for mates. Like rams, they could have slammed into each other at high speed, as shown below. It would take skulls three to ten inches thick to keep the animals' brains from being scrambled! The dinosaurs also had strong necks. They held the heads straight when the dinosaurs hit head-on.

Boneheads came in many sizes. One was no larger than a turkey. Another was about as big as a grown person. *Pachycephalosaurus* was probably the largest, but that is really a guess. All that scientists have found is a skull more than two feet long. They say that a bonehead with a skull that big would have been nearly 20 feet long. That is the length of an average living room.

One bonehead has a special claim to fame. That is the cat-sized *Micropachycephalosaurus* (MY-crow-pack-ee-SEF-uh-low-saw-rus). It has the longest name of any dinosaur.

# Winner Take All

Scientists base some of their ideas about bonehead dinosaurs on what they know about animals like these bighorn sheep. During the breeding season, male sheep fight over the females. After pushing and shoving each other, two males back away. Then they charge and crash head-on. After several crashes, one of the males walks away. The winner takes a mate. Scientists think the bonehead dinosaurs may have had similar battles.

# The Walking Tanks

One group of dinosaurs looked like walking tanks. These creatures were the *ankylosaurs* (an-KYLE-uh-sahrs), the "stiffened lizards." One of the best-known of the group was *Ankylosaurus.* At 25 feet long and 6 feet wide, the 10,000-pound creature was even bigger than a station wagon.

From head to tail, Ankylosaurus was covered with thick, bony plates. The plates were close together and covered by leathery skin. Short spikes protected the animal's sides. Its head was so well covered with plates that it looked as if it were wearing a helmet. Small plates protected its eyes and nose.

Ankylosaurus was a peaceful plant eater. Its armor was for protection against meat-eating enemies. It must have been a tough dinosaur to attack. A hungry meat eater might have wound up with a mouthful of broken teeth if it tried to bite through the "tank's" plates.

If the meat eater got near the armored dinosaur's rear end, it was in for a painful surprise. Ankylosaurus's tail ended in a round chunk of solid bone and looked like a war club (see the photo below, right). One smack from that club might have broken an attacker's leg or jaw. A crippled meat eater might have starved if it couldn't hunt or eat very well.

When Ankylosaurus was attacked, it probably crouched down so that its stomach touched the ground. That position would have protected its soft belly from the teeth and claws of its enemy.

If a meat eater flipped it over, however, the plant eater was defenseless. It could not turn itself right side up. And it may not have been able to swing its tail at its enemy. An attacker could easily kill it. Maybe that is how many ankylosaurs died. Most of the fossils of these dinosaurs were found upside down.

Ankylosaurus lived in western North America, but its armored relatives lived all over the world. One of them lived in China. It looked like the American ankylosaur, but with a few differences. It was only about 12 feet long, and it was more lightly built than Ankylosaurus. The club on its tail was flat and had a sharp edge. It looked more like a battle-ax than a war club, and probably it was used like one.

Other kinds of ankylosaurs had no tail clubs at all. But they weren't defenseless. One kind had sharp spines like those on a stegosaur's tail (see pages 40-41). Sometimes those spines ran in rows along the creatures' backs. Another kind had a mixture of bony spines, plates, knobs, and bumps all over its body.

The walking tanks were very successful dinosaurs. They were around for about 60 million years and were one of the last dinosaur families to die out.

*This solid club of bone was at the end of Ankylosaurus's tail and was the animal's main weapon. The club was probably covered by thick plates that were a lot like the ones on a turtle's shell.*

# Living Armor

Ankylosaurs were not the only animals to grow their own armor. The modern armadillo also has built-in protection. It has hard plates that overlap to cover its body. It also has plates on its head and tail. The plates are made of horn, a substance similar to fingernail. But, unlike Ankylosaurus, some armadillos don't lie flat on the ground when they are threatened. They can curl up into balls to hide their soft bellies when a coyote or other predator attacks.

# The Ostrich Dinosaurs

Which dinosaurs looked like ostriches, ran as fast as ostriches, and laid eggs like ostriches? The "ostrich dinosaurs," of course. *Ornithomimus* (or-nith-uh-MY-mus), pictured at the far right, was one of them. It was about 8 feet tall and 15 feet long. Ostriches are also about 8 feet tall.

Fossil skeletons prove that the ostrich dinosaurs really did look a lot like ostriches. They had small heads on top of long, skinny necks. They also had long, powerful back legs and hollow bones. They walked and ran on their hind legs. Their front legs were only good for grabbing things.

Ostrich dinosaurs' eyes were enormous and probably helped them spot food or enemies from far away. Their brains were large, too. Scientists think that the ostrich dinosaurs were among the smartest of the dinosaurs. Unlike most other dinosaurs, ostrich dinosaurs had no teeth. Instead, they had horny beaks that looked almost like the beaks of ostriches.

These dinosaurs acted like the big birds, too. Ornithomimus and the others seem to have been very fast runners. Their shin bones were longer than their thigh bones. This tells scientists that, like modern ostriches, ostrich dinosaurs were built for speed. They could have run from enemies at nearly 50 miles per hour.

To be that fast, these dinosaurs had to have a lot of energy. They may have been warmblooded. Scientists know that warmblooded animals often can be more active than cold-blooded ones (see pages 18-19).

Although ostrich dinosaurs looked a lot like ostriches, there were many differences. For one, the dinosaurs were reptiles, not birds. They had leathery skin instead of feathers. They had feet with three toes, and they had long tails that helped them keep their balance when they ran. Ostriches have only two toes

Ostrich

**Ornithomimus
(or-nith-uh-MY-mus)**

on each foot, and no bony tails at all. Look closely at the picture of the ostrich dinosaur. It shows a creature with long arms and hands with three fingers. Now look at the ostrich. Instead of arms, it has only short, useless wings.

Scientists are not sure what the ostrich dinosaurs ate. They could have torn open ant colonies with their claws and licked up the insects with their tongues. They may have used their hands to pull fruit or leaves from tree branches. Or maybe they ate small lizards or mammals. Ostriches eat both plants and meat. Perhaps the ostrich dinosaurs did too.

One interesting idea is that these dinosaurs stole eggs. Fossil hunters in the Gobi Desert of Mongolia found the remains of an ostrich dinosaur in a nest with broken dinosaur eggs. The scientists think that the egg stealers shoveled sand away from the buried eggs with their hands. Then they pulled the eggs out of the nests with their clawed fingers. Using their sharp beaks, they cracked the eggshells open and slurped up the contents.

If an angry parent attacked, the ostrich dinosaur tried to run away on its speedy hind legs. But not all of the egg stealers were able to get away in time. The little one found in Mongolia appears to have been killed while eating the eggs. Its skull had been smashed flat, perhaps by a larger dinosaur's foot.

# The Terrible Claw

One hundred million years ago, a killer ran free across what is now Montana. It was armed with razor-sharp teeth and deadly claws five inches long. And it would attack animals several times its size. That superbly equipped hunter was *Deinonychus* (dine-ON-ick-us), the "terrible claw."

The creature's terrible claws were really terrible toes. The second toe of each hind foot was curved like a claw and had a long, sharp toenail. When Deinonychus ran, it held these claws up off the ground. That way they would not become dull. When it attacked, its claws swung down into action.

The terrible-claw dinosaurs were built for hunting. They probably were swift runners, for they had strong hind legs. They had large brains that helped them outsmart their prey. They had big eyes that might have helped them find food in the dark. They had hands that were perfectly shaped for holding prey, and they had long tails that helped them keep their balance when they ran. They also were probably warmblooded.

Deinonychus was barely five feet tall. It weighed about 175 pounds. And it was only nine feet long from the end of its snout to the tip of its tail. But what it lacked in size it made up for in fierceness.

When Deinonychus attacked, it jumped at its prey to knock it down. Then it hopped from one foot to the other, ripping into the animal with its free foot. Since the claws could slash downwards and backwards, they must have made great wounds in the victim's hide.

To keep from losing its balance while struggling with prey, Deinonychus used its tail. Long, very stiff tendons grew out of the tail bones. They ran the length of the tail and helped stiffen it. With a stiff tail for support,

Deinonychus could balance itself better when using its feet to fight.

Deinonychus hardly seemed big enough to kill a really large animal by itself. It might have gotten help from others of its kind. Scientists believe that these dinosaurs traveled and hunted in packs like wolves. Together, several of these fierce meat eaters could have

**Deinonychus
(dine-ON-ick-us)**

## Terrible Hands

Deinonychus is called the "terrible claw" because of its huge toenails. Its cousin, *Deinocheirus* (die-nuh-KYE-rus), is called the "terrible hand" because of its huge hands and fingernails. Its arms were longer than a human. Its hands could easily reach around a person. Its claws, which were 8 to 10 inches long, could tear right through many other animals' skins. So far, only the bones shown here—plus a few others—have been found. They were dug up in Mongolia in 1965.

killed a dinosaur several times their size.

In 1964, evidence of such a battle was found. The bones of a large plant eater were discovered next to the remains of four or five Deinonychus skeletons near Billings, Montana. The giant may have killed several of the attackers. Then it died from wounds made by the other members of the pack.

61

# A Fight to the Death

The *Velociraptor* (vuh-lahs-ih-RAP-tor) thought it would be easy to steal the baby *Protoceratops* (pro-toe-SEHR-uh-tops) for dinner. It had taken these creatures from nests many times before. Often it had sneaked in and escaped before the parents could chase it away. Even when a Protoceratops had attacked, the Velociraptor had had no trouble in winning the fight. It was bigger than a Protoceratops, and it had long, sharp claws.

The Velociraptor had barely begun to eat when a Protoceratops charged at it from behind a nearby tree. The Protoceratops was a plant eater and didn't have long claws or teeth. But its big head was covered with hard, bony plates that curved up in back like a shield. And it had a parrotlike beak with a sharp point. The point could poke through thick skin.

**Protoceratops**
**(pro-toe-SEHR-uh-tops)**

*The scientist at left digs very carefully as he uncovers the fossils of two dinosaurs that died while fighting. The neck and skull of a Velociraptor lie next to the man's left hand. His right hand is partly hidden behind the skull of a Protoceratops. The painting above shows the creatures in about the same position as in the photograph.*

Giving a swift kick with one of its feet, the Velociraptor tore into the Protoceratops. But at the same time, the Protoceratops swung its head down in an attack of its own. The two creatures were badly wounded. The Protoceratops's beak stuck into the other's chest. The Velociraptor seems to have caught one of its claws in its enemy's head. They died with their bodies locked together.

Millions of years later, scientists found them just as they had died. The fossils were discovered in Mongolia in 1971.

The story about the fight between the Velociraptor and the Protoceratops is based on a guess. Scientists know that the two skeletons were stuck to each other. And they know that Protoceratops built nests to hold their eggs and babies. But they don't know for sure that Protoceratops fought other animals to defend their nests or young. However, many modern animals do defend their nests and babies, and it is possible that Protoceratops did, too. If they really did, then we can be pretty sure that the one in the photograph was fighting the Velociraptor to protect its young.

The stuck-together fossils were a very exciting find. So was the first Protoceratops egg. It was discovered in 1922. Until then, no one knew how dinosaurs produced their young. People knew that dinosaurs were reptiles and that most reptiles lay eggs. Dinosaurs probably did, too. Still, people were not sure.

A group from the American Museum of Natural History in New York City made the first find. They were hunting for fossils in Mongolia's Gobi Desert. When one of the group reported finding eggs, the others thought he was joking. They said he had found only rocks shaped like eggs. But when everyone joined the search, they found three oval objects about eight inches long. They were shaped just like reptile eggs. Even more eggs appeared to be buried in a block of stone.

Later, 13 eggs were chipped out of the stone. The eggs formed a circle, which made the scientists think that the eggs had been laid in a nest. Inside two of the eggs were Protoceratops skeletons, proof that these really were dinosaur eggs.

**Velociraptor
(vuh-lahs-ih-RAP-tor)**

# Horns and Frills

I t is easy to pick out the *ceratopsids* (sehr-uh-TOP-sids) in a museum. They are the dinosaurs with the big heads and horns. Their name means "horned faces." Their skulls curved up in back into a wide frill. The frill is shaped a little like a Japanese fan. Including that frill, the head made up almost a third of the animal's length. Some skulls measured nearly nine feet long.

Nearly a dozen different dinosaurs were in this group. Their best-known ancestor, Protoceratops, lived in Mongolia. Some other early relatives have turned up in the western mountains of Canada and the United States. When the ceratopsids were alive, that area was a low plain. It was next to a sea that stretched from Canada to Mexico.

The ceratopsids, which evolved late in the Cretaceous period, were the last dinosaurs to appear on earth. They were shaped like rhinoceroses. The largest were a bit longer than a large car. Others were less than half that long. When the Age of Dinosaurs ended (see pages 78-79), they were among the last creatures to become extinct.

*Monoclonius* (mon-uh-CLONE-ee-us), whose name means "single twig," looked less scary than many of its cousins. It had a single, long horn on its snout (below, right). But that was all. Over its eyebrows, where some other ceratopsids had more horns, it had only little bumps. At the very top of its frill, two spikes curved out like upside-down horns. Scientists are still trying to find out what they were for.

*Styracosaurus* (sty-RACK-uh-saw-rus), the "spiked lizard," also had only one horn. But its large frill held giant spikes that really made it look dangerous (below). To scare off an enemy, all Styracosaurus had to do was bend down its head. That would make the frill stand straight up and look even larger and more threatening.

The frills also protected the animals if they were attacked. The Velociraptor that attacked Protoceratops (see pages 62-63) found that out when its claw got stuck in the animal's head.

Defense was only one purpose the frills served. They also held one end of the animals' extra-large jaw muscles. These dinosaurs

**Styracosaurus (sty-RACK-uh-saw-rus)**

# Safe in a Circle

Did the horned dinosaurs behave like modern musk oxen when they were in danger? Maybe. When threatened, musk oxen form a circle (below) with their young in the middle. The adults face outward. Maybe the horned dinosaurs protected their families the same way. Like the oxen, the horned dinosaurs were plant eaters and traveled in groups. A tight circle of the creatures would have made good protection for the entire group. These dinosaurs did have another form of defense: their horns. Even a single adult could put up a good fight.

needed strong jaws to cut up the tough leaves of palm trees.

Different kinds of frills may have helped the males and females identify each other. Right now, though, scientists have no way of proving that theory.

One thing about the horns and frills is certain. They were really used. Fossils of some ceratopsids have turned up with scarred and broken horns. Some fossilized frills also have patches of extra bone. These patches show where the frills had healed from wounds.

**Monoclonius**
**(mon-uh-CLONE-ee-us)**

# The Last Horned Face

Late in the Age of Dinosaurs, among the most common dinosaurs in western North America were *Triceratops* (try-SEHR-uh-tops). They were the creatures with "three-horned faces." More than half the fossils found in parts of the West are of Triceratops.

These animals were heavier than the heaviest elephants and longer than pickup trucks. Their thick, curved horns were three feet long.

The horns were useful for fighting for mates and for defense. A single Triceratops could drive off a predator as large and dangerous as Tyrannosaurus rex (see pages 68-69).

Triceratops did not kill other animals for food. Instead, it ate plants. First, it snapped off the tops of palms and other short trees with its sharp beak. Then it chomped the plants into tiny pieces with its 640 teeth.

Some artists have shown Triceratops with a long mouth, like that of an alligator. But a mouth that big couldn't have held in much food. A lot of food would have fallen out when the animal tried to chew. In more recent art, shown here, Triceratops has a short mouth and large cheeks (for holding in the food).

**Triceratops (try-SEHR-uh-tops)**

# The Tyrant King

*A technician (left) at the Smithsonian Institution in Washington, D.C., puts the finishing touches on a cast of a Tyrannosaurus skull. A cast is a copy of a fossil, often made of fiberglass. Casts are made so that museums can have skeletons to show, since there are not enough real skeletons to go around.*

**Triceratops
(try-SEHR-uh-tops)**

I magine a two-legged, meat-eating dinosaur tall enough to look into the upstairs windows of a house. Picture it flashing teeth and claws as long and sharp as carving knives, then attacking its prey with fury.

Sounds like a creature out of a horror movie, doesn't it? But such an animal really did exist. It was a dinosaur named *Tyrannosaurus rex* (tie-RAN-uh-saw-rus recks), which means "king tyrant lizard." A tyrant is a leader who rules his subjects without pity or mercy. Because Tyrannosaurus rex was the biggest meat eater ever to walk the land, it is said to be the king of the meat eaters.

Tyrannosaurus was more than 50 feet long. That is longer than the trailer of a big truck on a highway. It was about 20 feet high and weighed nearly eight tons.

The dinosaur's head was enormous. The one in the photograph to the left looks big enough to swallow a large dog whole. Each eye socket is as big as a soccer ball. The jaws are lined with 60 dagger-sharp teeth. The largest teeth are about six inches long and have serrated cutting edges like steak knives.

Teeth like these are not for chewing food. They are for puncturing and slicing. After killing its victim, Tyrannosaurus probably held it to the ground with its hind feet. Then it bit off big chunks of meat and swallowed them whole. After eating, Tyrannosaurus might have lain down near the carcass and slept.

Tyrannosaurus had plenty of animals to choose for dinner, but some were easier to hunt than others. Horned dinosaurs like Triceratops could put up a real fight. As in the painting to the left, a Triceratops could use its horns to spear an attacker. Ankylosaurs were not any easier to attack. They could have smashed their war-club tails into Tyrannosaurus's head and legs.

Duckbills and the few long-necked plant eaters that were still around were probably Tyrannosaurus's favorite food. They were large, slow, and nearly defenseless—just the right kind of meal for a hungry meat eater.

Some scientists say that Tyrannosaurus was too big and heavy to be an active hunter. They think it moved too slowly to fight Triceratops or to go running after a duckbill. They believe that it was a scavenger like a vulture, feeding on dead animals.

Other scientists think just the opposite. They agree that Tyrannosaurus was too heavy to run quickly. But they add that its prey did not move very fast either. They also point out that the meat eater's teeth are not the right shape for scavenging.

**Tyrannosaurus (tie-RAN-uh-saw-rus)**

# The Fierce Family

**Daspletosaurus
(das-PLEE-tuh-saw-rus)**

Tyrannosaurus rex was not the only giant meat-eating dinosaur. It had relatives all over the world. A Canadian cousin, *Daspletosaurus* (das-PLEE-tuh-saw-rus), looked a lot like Tyrannosaurus rex, only smaller (right). Other relatives lived in Mongolia and Egypt. The one in Egypt had a six-foot-high fin on its back. The fin may have served as a radiator to keep the creature cool in the desert.

"Rex" and all its cousins are called *tyrannosaurs*. They all had huge bodies, but tiny arms and hands with only two fingers each. Scientists are not sure how the tyrannosaurs used their arms. They were too small to hold prey and too short to use for scratching.

Maybe the arms helped the animals get up from the ground after lying down. First, the dinosaurs would dig their front claws into the dirt. Then they would push up with their strong legs. Without the claws on their hands acting as brakes, their heavy heads might have slid along the ground and they might not have been able to get up.

Once up, the tyrannosaurs probably waddled like giant ducks when they walked. Even so, their strides stretched up to 14 feet. They also stuck their tails straight out rather than let them drag on the ground. That helped to balance the weight of their heavy heads.

Though they were all related, tyrannosaurs were not friendly to each other. They may have fought for food or territory. We think this because one fossil tyrannosaur skeleton was found with broken ribs and a punctured jaw. The wounds appear to have been made by the teeth of another tyrannosaur.

This life-sized picture of a carnosaur's tooth (below) shows just how dangerous these meat eaters were. The edges of the tooth are notched, and they cut like the blade of a steak knife. This tooth probably came from an early relative of Daspletosaurus (left) and Tyrannosaurus rex. It was found in Tanzania.

Champsosaurus
(CHAMP-suh-saw-rus)

# Birds with Teeth

Late in the Age of Dinosaurs the world was full of birds. Two of them were *Hesperornis* (hess-purr-OR-niss) (3) and *Ichthyornis* (ick-thee-OR-niss) (1). They both lived around an inland sea that covered parts of western North America from Mexico to Canada. Like Archaeopteryx (see pages 46-47), these birds had teeth and feathers. But unlike that first bird, Ichthyornis could fly very well. And Hesperornis was a strong swimmer and diver.

Fossils of Hesperornis, which means "western bird," have been found in Kansas, Alberta, and other parts of midwestern and western North America. Hesperornis had no wings, but it had feathers and therefore was a real bird. It grew up to six feet long and looked like a giant loon (4), and like a loon, it had webbed feet that helped it swim.

Scientists think Hesperornis spent most of its time in the water diving for fish. It used its small, sharp teeth to spear the fish. Hesperornis laid eggs, so it probably came to the shore to nest and raise its young.

Ichthyornis looked like a sea gull (2) with teeth. Like a gull, Ichthyornis lived on shore. It probably flew out over the water in search of fish. When it spotted one, it dived into the water and snapped up the meal with its flat, toothed beak. Scientists named the bird for its diet. *Ichthyornis* means "fish bird."

What really interests scientists is the way Ichthyornis flew. It had a large breastbone to which large flight muscles were attached. With these muscles, it could flap its wings and take off and land almost anywhere, anytime, as some pterosaurs did. It didn't have to wait for breezes or warm air currents so it could soar. It didn't have to climb a tree or a cliff and glide to the ground as Archaeopteryx may have done. It was the first bird we know of that could really fly!

2

1. Ichthyornis
   (ick-thee-OR-niss)
2. Ring-billed gull
3. Hesperornis
   (hess-purr-OR-niss)
4. Loon

1

4

3

# Quetzalcoatlus

Quetzalcoatlus had about four times the wingspan of today's largest land birds, the condors. Andean and California condors have wingspans measuring between 9 and 10 feet.

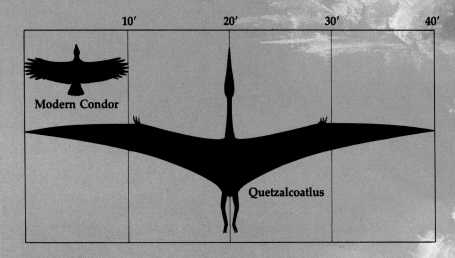

| 10' | 20' | 30' | 40' |
|---|---|---|---|

Modern Condor

Quetzalcoatlus

Wonderful, incredible, and scary! There is no better way to describe the largest flying creature of all time. That was *Quetzalcoatlus* (ket-sul-co-AT-lus), named for the feathered god of the ancient Aztec Indians of Mexico. Its bones were found in Texas in the 1970's.

Quetzalcoatlus was not a bird. It was a pterosaur, a kind of reptile. It was related to the flying reptiles that first appeared millions of years earlier (see pages 48-49).

With a span of about 40 feet, Quetzalcoatlus's wings were as wide as a small airplane's wings. Quetzalcoatlus soared like a vulture on rising columns of warm air. Though it lived inland away from the ocean, it may have fed on fish it scooped out of rivers. Some people think it walked across mud flats and poked its long beak into the mud to find food.

Once Quetzalcoatlus landed, getting back into the air could have been a problem. It couldn't flap its wings and take off the way most birds do. Its wings were so long they would have scraped the ground. And it couldn't soar from high cliffs, as some seabirds do, because the land where it lived was flat.

If the huge soarer had to wait on the ground for a strong wind to lift it up, it might have been in trouble on a still day. Stranded on the ground, it would have been an easy target for predators on the prowl.

Maybe Quetzalcoatlus stretched out its wings and ran downhill until it gained enough speed to take off. That idea is not as strange as it seems. Albatrosses and hang-glider pilots sometimes do the same thing.

# The Real Nessie?

Did creatures like Elasmosaurus really survive for 65 million years and surface as Scotland's Loch Ness Monster? Some people think so. They point to pictures like this one, taken in 1934, as proof that the monster exists. Other people think the monster story is just a legend. They say that the picture shows some modern animal. Still, scientists and others continue to watch the 25-mile-long Loch Ness. They want to know for sure if there really is a monster.

# Sea Monsters

Chasmosaurus (KAZ-muh-saw-rus)

Skull of Phobosuchus

Phobosuchus (foe-buh-SUE-kus)

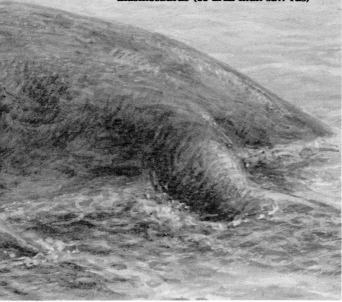

**Elasmosaurus (ee-LAZ-muh-saw-rus)**

**Y**ou could probably lie down inside the jaws of a *Phobosuchus* (foe-buh-SUE-kus) skeleton. This forty-foot-long "horror croco-dile" lived in swamps in Montana and other western states. It was the largest crocodile that ever lived. Its head was as large as an adult human being (left, top).

The horror crocodile wasn't a dinosaur, but it hunted dinosaurs when it had a chance. The young *Chasmosaurus* (KAZ-muh-saw-rus) dino-saur in the painting (left, center) is probably eight to nine feet long, but it looks small next to the horror crocodile that is about to attack it. The horror crocodile's big teeth could cut right through the Chasmosaurus's skin.

In the oceans, other swimming giants were content with a diet of fish. *Elasmosaurus* (ee-LAZ-muh-saw-rus) was the largest member of the family of reptiles called *plesiosaurs* (PLEE-zee-uh-sahrs) (left, bottom). It was about as long as a big school bus. Remains of those creatures have been found on every continent, including icy Antarctica.

Elasmosaurus probably swam on the surface of the sea. It had small flippers, so it probably paddled along slowly. It snapped up any fish that swam or jumped too close to its long neck. Holding on to a wiggling fish was easy, because Elasmosaurus had very sharp teeth.

Chewing the fish may not have been easy, though. Elasmosaurus's teeth were shaped for puncturing, not grinding. Some scientists say that the creature swallowed stones to help grind up its dinner. Some dinosaurs may also have done that (see pages 28-29). Other scien-tists think that Elasmosaurus swallowed stones to add to its weight. Extra weight would help it dive more easily.

Today, all the plesiosaurs have died out, but the crocodiles live on. Phobosuchus itself is gone, but its smaller descendants are still around. They live in warm swamps and rivers around the world.

A few people believe that the legendary Loch Ness Monster is an Elasmosaurus, or one of the other plesiosaurs. Every now and then, someone claims to see one in Loch Ness, the deep, cold lake in Scotland that has given the creature its name.

# Death of the Dinosaurs

Maybe small mammals ate all the dinosaurs' eggs. Maybe diseases killed both the animals and the plants. Every theory starts with the word *maybe*. The truth is, we just don't know why the dinosaurs and many other animals and plants died.

Maybe no single cause killed them. The earth was changing, as it always is. So were

For more than 140 million years, dinosaurs and other reptiles ruled the earth. They were everywhere—on the land, in the air, and in the sea. Suddenly, life on the whole planet changed. Every dinosaur, every pterosaur, and every large sea reptile died. Over half of the earth's animals and plants became extinct. The change may have taken a hundred years, a million years, or more. We do not know. But, compared to the time those reptiles had been living on earth, the change was sudden.

Why this happened is a mystery that scientists have been trying to solve for years. Astronomers know that exploding stars give off light and deadly radiation. Perhaps a star exploded too near our solar system. The radiation might have killed many animals and plants. It could also have changed the climate. The earth might have become too cold for many plants and animals to survive.

Other scientists have found evidence that an asteroid (a very small planet) might have hit the earth and exploded. They say that dust from the explosion kept sunlight from reaching the earth for years. Without sunlight, most plants died. Because the plants died, the plant-eating animals died. Then, without any prey, the meat eaters died.

Some scientists say that the flowering plants were at fault. These plants appeared near the end of the Age of Dinosaurs. Animals eating them might have died from food poisoning.

Maybe the problem was the weather. For millions of years, the earth had been warm all year. Now there were seasons. If the weather turned too cold, the dinosaurs might have died from exposure. They had no fur or feathers to keep them warm. If it got too hot, the dinosaurs' eggs might have been cooked before they could hatch.

the dinosaurs and other animals. One group would die out, and another group would appear to take its place. Maybe too many changes were happening at one time for all the animals to adapt to. The birds made it. So did the early mammals. Even many fish, turtles, lizards, snakes, and crocodiles survived. But that time the dinosaurs did not.

*According to one theory, this Ankylosaurus and the other dinosaurs became extinct when radiation from an exploding star turned the earth cold.*

# A New Day Dawns

Without dinosaurs, the world seemed empty. No herds of giants browsed the treetops. No sharp-toothed meat eaters chased prey. No thick-skulled "boneheads" battled for mates. But not all animal life was dead. Birds were still around. So were crocodiles and snakes. And almost hidden in the shadows were the tiny creatures that would take over the earth. These were the mammals.

There were not many mammals in the first years after the death of the dinosaurs. Most of them were about as small as mice. The largest was about the size of a bulldog.

Among the really small mammals were the ancestors of the three main groups known today. One group, called *monotremes* (MAHN-uh-treems), laid eggs. The only monotremes alive now are the duck-billed platypus and the spiny anteaters. The duck-billed platypus lives in Australia, and the spiny anteaters live in Australia and New Guinea.

Another group carried their young in pouches. They were the *marsupials* (mar-SUE-pea-uls) (1). The best-known marsupials today are the opossum, common in the United States, and the kangaroo and wallaby, found in Australia.

The third group carried their young inside their bodies until they were born. They are called *placentals* (pluh-SENT-uls) (2, 3, 4). Today, the placentals live everywhere—in the air, in the sea, and on the land. They include many, many kinds of animals, from bats to whales, cats to cows, pandas to people. One of the smallest placentals is a shrew only 1½ inches long. The largest is the blue whale—nearly 100 feet long.

Is the day of the mammals now coming to an end? Some people think that might be true. Air and water pollution and the destruction of wildlife habitat are lowering the populations of many kinds of mammals. These problems kill more than just mammals. They also hurt fish, birds, and other creatures. We must learn how to take better care of our planet.

80

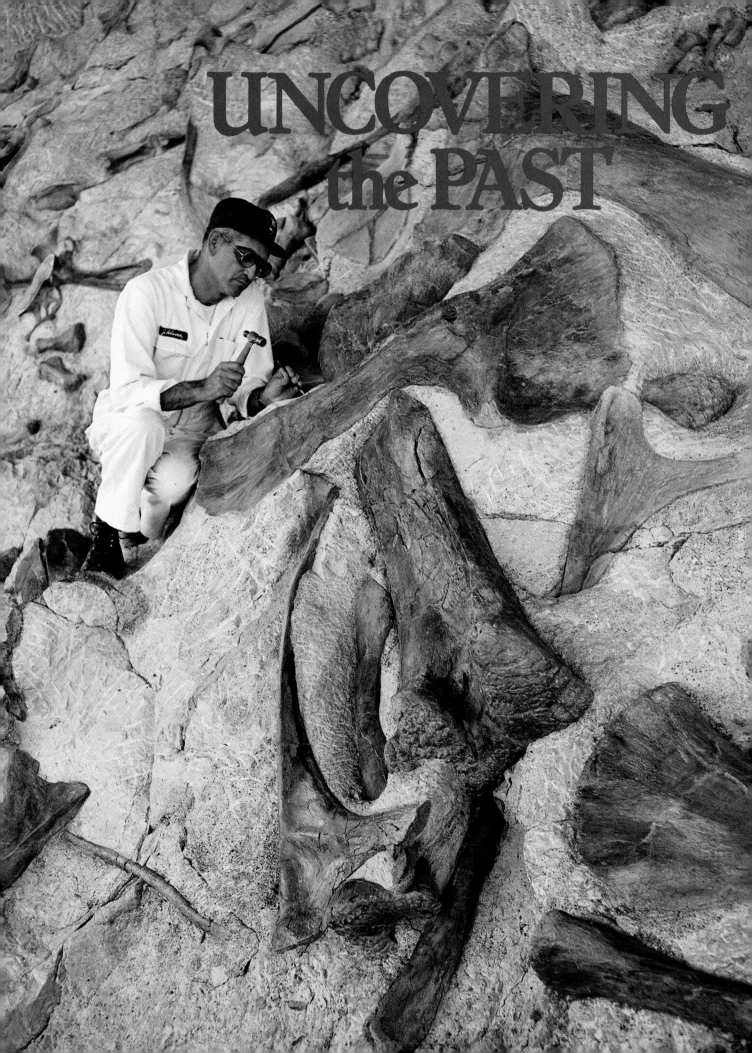

# UNCOVERING the PAST

The last dinosaurs died about 65 million years ago, but they are not forgotten. Paleontologists make new discoveries every year. Nearly 100 new kinds of dinosaurs have been found in the last 20 years. Some of these haven't even been named yet.

Dinosaur bones are not the only kinds of fossils that paleontologists look for. The remains of other animals and plants are just as important to find. That is because every fossil may be a clue that helps solve mysteries about what life and the environment were like millions of years ago.

Not every living thing becomes a fossil after it dies. Only a few of the billions and billions of plants and animals that have existed since life began have become fossils. That is because fossils form only under special conditions. And when fossils do form, changes in the rocks may destroy the fossils before they are found.

Paleontologists are not the only people who find dinosaur bones and other fossils. Farmers, miners, construction workers—and kids—do too! A 12-year-old English girl was the first person to discover an ichthyosaur skeleton.

Some good places to look for fossils are in caves or along riverbanks, in rock quarries or sand and gravel pits, and at construction sites. Fossils may also be found in coal mines and along roads where they are cut through hills and mountains. Another good spot is at the shore where waves have worn away the land.

Finding fossils takes a lot of time and work. Usually, nothing of scientific value is found. But sometimes a fossil hunter makes a great discovery. Imagine digging up the remains of a plant or animal never before seen by humans. That would be the thrill of a lifetime!

*Uncovering the past means a lot of hard digging for workers like the one at Dinosaur National Monument (left). Part of their job is to separate the bones of different dinosaurs that are mixed together. It may take years before scientists can put together a complete skeleton like that of Deinonychus (above).*

# Buried Treasures

Hunting for fossils is like hunting for buried treasure. Using a map, scientists go to where the rocks are old enough to contain dinosaur bones. They spend days searching the ground for clues like bits of bone, teeth, or claws. Many times they find nothing. Any bone fragments they find may be signs that more of a skeleton lies just a few inches under ground or higher up on a hillside. Often, pieces of bone that scientists find have been washed down out of the hills by rain.

*(Right) Fossils are often found in rugged areas like South Dakota's badlands. Here wind and water slowly wear away the tons of rock that cover ancient bones.*

*(Below) In 1964, while searching for fossils in Montana, Dr. John Ostrom discovered this large claw. The rest of the skeleton of Deinonychus (see pages 60-61) was only a few inches under ground.*

# Freeing the Fossils

Finding fossils of dinosaurs is only the beginning. Next comes digging them up. Sometimes the bones are covered by only a few inches or feet of earth. But often they are buried beneath tons of hard rock. The workers must dig carefully to keep from breaking the fossils. As they dig, scientists make a drawing of where the bones lie in relation to each other. The drawing is a map of the dinosaur dig. It is important later on for putting the bones back together or for recreating the digging site for display in a museum.

(Below) *Wrapped and numbered, heavy fossils must be lifted by a crane and put on a truck. The numbers help scientists put the bones back together the way they were when they were found.*

(Above) *Digging up large fossils requires picks and jackhammers— and sometimes dynamite. As much rock as possible must be removed from the fossil without cutting into the fossil itself.*

(Far left) *Smaller fossils are chipped slowly out of the rock with chisels and cleaned off with soft brushes. Pieces that break are carefully glued back together.*

(Left) *Large fossils are covered with a cast made of burlap and plaster. The cast keeps the fragile fossils from breaking when they are carried back to the lab.*

# Return of the Dinosaurs

In the laboratory, months or even years are spent preparing the fossils brought back from a dig. All the rock surrounding each bone must be removed. Large chunks of rock are chipped off with a hammer and chisel. Small areas of rock are sometimes "sanded" off by an abrasive powder sprayed under high pressure. Individual grains of sand are removed with a needle. When a fossil bone is clean, it is painted with a clear liquid that hardens when it dries. This covering protects the fossil from humidity.

(Right) *This skeleton of an Antrodemus is part of a large display of dinosaur skeletons at the Smithsonian Institution in Washington, D.C. (next page).*

(Below) *Cleaned bones must be sorted and put back together. Broken bones are mended, and missing bones are replaced with copies made of plaster or fiberglass.*

(Above) *Patient picking and poking are needed to remove a skull from its rocky tomb. This Allosaurus skull was found at Dinosaur National Monument, Utah.*

# WHERE to SEE DINOSAURS

Pictures of dinosaurs are fun to look at, but nothing beats seeing a real dinosaur skeleton.

Many museums and universities have at least one dinosaur skeleton on display. They may also have models that show what the creatures looked like when they were alive. A few museums have really large exhibits, with fossils of several animals set up for you to see. Here are some of the largest such museums in the United States and Canada:

American Museum of Natural History—
New York, New York

Carnegie Museum of Natural History—
Pittsburgh, Pennsylvania

Denver Museum of Natural History—
Denver, Colorado

Field Museum of Natural History—
Chicago, Illinois

Milwaukee Public Museum—
Milwaukee, Wisconsin

National Museum of Natural History
(Smithsonian Institution)—
Washington, D.C.

National Museum of Natural Sciences
(National Museums of Canada)—
Ottawa, Ontario, Canada

Natural History Museum of Los Angeles
County—Los Angeles, California

Peabody Museum of Natural History
(Yale University)—
New Haven, Connecticut

Royal Ontario Museum—
Toronto, Ontario, Canada

Tyrrell Museum of Paleontology—
Drumheller, Alberta, Canada

University of Utah—Salt Lake City, Utah

It is exciting, too, to see the footprints left by dinosaurs. Some museums have dug up the rocks containing the tracks and put them on display. There are also places where you can see the tracks right where the dinosaurs made them. Here are the two best-known sites:

Glen Rose, Texas

Dinosaur State Park—
Rocky Hill, Connecticut

Most fossil hunters do not want sightseers in the way when they are trying to dig up fragile bones and other fossils. But there are at least two places where the public is welcome to see a real "dig" in progress. There you can watch as professionals carefully cut away the rock to uncover the fossilized bones. Those two places are:

Dinosaur National Monument—
near Vernal, Utah

Dinosaur Provincial Park—
near Brooks, Alberta, Canada

# ABOUT the ARTISTS

Paintings and drawings of dinosaurs help bring to life that strange age of long ago. In this book we show artwork done for the National Wildlife Federation by some of today's best dinosaur artists. We have also included other art that we think is outstanding.

Single pieces of art came from these four artists: **Robert Byrd, Alex Ebel, Walter Ferguson, and John Gurche.** Most of our illustrations—more than three dozen of them—came from the following six artists:

**Biruta Akerbergs** is a freelance artist and Museum Specialist for the Smithsonian Institution. Her work has appeared in many books and magazines, including *Ranger Rick.* She also drew the illustrations for another National Wildlife Federation book, *Earth's Amazing Animals.*

**John D. Dawson** is another freelance artist whose drawings have appeared in *Ranger Rick.* His illustrations have been used by many book and magazine publishers and have appeared in an encyclopedia and in publications of leading zoos and the U.S. Department of the Interior.

**Mark Hallett** used to teach biological illustration at the Natural History Museum of Los Angeles County. He has also painted murals and prepared exhibits for zoos and museums. In addition, he has written and illustrated magazine articles on prehistoric life.

**Eleanor M. Kish** is one of Canada's leading artists. In recent years, she has painted many pictures of nature. The paintings we used first appeared in another book, *A Vanished World—The Dinosaurs of Western Canada.* It was published by Canada's National Museum of Natural Sciences. The museum also showed these paintings in an exhibit about dinosaurs.

**Charles R. Knight** (1874-1953) is probably the most famous American artist of prehistoric life. He created close to 1,000 pieces of art. Even today artists study his works. You can see many of his paintings and murals in the leading natural history museums in the United States.

**Rudolph F. Zallinger** received a Pulitzer Prize for his outstanding mural, *Age of Reptiles.* That and his *Age of Mammals* mural are in the Peabody Museum of Natural History at Yale University. He now teaches drawing and painting at the University of Hartford (Connecticut) and is an artist-in-residence at the Peabody Museum.

**Triceratops model at the Smithsonian Institution, Washington, D.C.**

# INDEX

# ILLUSTRATION CREDITS

Cover: John D. Dawson. Page 1: Rudolph F. Zallinger. 2-3: John D. Dawson. 4-5: *top row* (Pterodactylus) Biruta Akerbergs; (Hypacrosaurus) Eleanor M. Kish painting/National Museum of Natural Sciences, National Museums of Canada; (Parasaurolophus) Biruta Akerbergs; *second row* (Triceratops) Eleanor M. Kish painting/National Museum of Natural Sciences, National Museums of Canada; (Purgatorius) Mark Hallett; (Deinonychus and technician) William K. Sacco; *third row* (Protoceratops and Velociraptor) Mark Hallett; (Dryptosaurus) Charles R. Knight/Courtesy of the American Museum of Natural History; *fourth row* (Iguanodon) Rudolph F. Zallinger; (Ultrasaurus) Biruta Akerbergs; (Allosaurus) Charles R. Knight/Courtesy of the American Museum of Natural History; (Ornitholestes) Charles R. Knight/Courtesy of the American Museum of Natural History.

## INTRODUCTION TO DINOSAURS

Pages 6-7: John D. Dawson. 8: Rudolph F. Zallinger. 9: Biruta Akerbergs. 10: By courtesy of the Trustees, British Museum (Natural History). 10-11: Robert Byrd. 12-13: (top and middle) Courtesy of the American Museum of Natural History; (bottom) Peabody Museum of Natural History/Yale University. 13: Courtesy of the American Museum of Natural History. 14-15: John D. Dawson. 15: (bottom right) Biruta Akerbergs. 16-17: Eleanor M. Kish painting/National Museum of Natural Sciences, National Museums of Canada. 18-19: Charles R. Knight/Courtesy of the American Museum of Natural History. 20 & 21: Biruta Akerbergs.

## DAWN OF THE DINOSAURS

Pages 22-23: John D. Dawson. 24-25: Mark Hallett. 26: Laurence Pringle. 27: Mark Hallett; (inset) Wyman Meinzer. 28-29: Rudolph F. Zallinger. 29: George W. Calef. 30-31: Mark Hallett.

## TIME OF THE GIANTS

Pages 32-33: John D. Dawson. 34-35: Jen & Des Bartlett/Bruce Coleman, Inc. 35: Courtesy of the American Museum of Natural History. 36: Rudolph F. Zallinger. 37: Norman Myers/Bruce Coleman, Inc. 38: (left) Courtesy of Dr. José Bonaparte, Buenos Aires, Argentina; (right) Mark A. Philbrick. 38-39: Biruta Akerbergs. 40-41: Mark Hallett. 42-43: Charles R. Knight/Courtesy of the American Museum of Natural History. 43: Courtesy of the American Museum of Natural History. 44: Rudolph F. Zallinger. 45: Charles R. Knight/Courtesy of the American Museum of Natural History. 46-47: John R. Gurche. 48: E.R. Degginger/Earth Scenes. 48-49: Biruta Akerbergs. 49: Stanley Breeden.

## SEASONS OF CHANGE

Pages 50-51: John D. Dawson. 52: Museum of the Rockies, Montana State University. 52-53: Biruta Akerbergs. 54-55: Mark Hallett. 55: John S. Crawford. 56-57: (top) Rudolph F. Zallinger; (bottom) Courtesy of the American Museum of Natural History. 57: E.R. Degginger/Bruce Coleman, Inc. 58: George H. Harrison. 58-59: Rudolph F. Zallinger. 60-61: John D. Dawson. 61: Institute of Paleobiology, Warsaw, Poland. 62: Institute of Paleobiology, Warsaw, Poland. 62-63: Mark Hallett. 64: Rudolph F. Zallinger. 65: (top) S.D. MacDonald/National Museum of Natural Sciences, Canada; (bottom) Rudolph F. Zallinger. 66-67: Eleanor M. Kish painting/National Museum of Natural Sciences, National Museums of Canada. 68: Chip Clark. 68-69: Alex Ebel (from *Childcraft—The How and Why Library* © 1982 World Book, Inc.). 70-71: Eleanor M. Kish painting/National Museum of Natural Sciences, National Museums of Canada. 71: By courtesy of the Trustees, British Museum (Natural History). 72: Lynn Rogers. 72-73: Rudolph F. Zallinger. 73: (top) Olive Glasgow; (bottom) Rudolph F. Zallinger. 74-75: Biruta Akerbergs. 76: Wide World Photos. 76-77: (top) Walter Ferguson/Courtesy of the American Museum of Natural History; (bottom) Rudolph F. Zallinger. 77: Courtesy of the American Museum of Natural History. 78-79: Eleanor M. Kish painting/National Museum of Natural Sciences, National Museums of Canada. 80 & 81: Mark Hallett.

## UNCOVERING THE PAST

Page 82: National Park Service/U.S. Department of the Interior. 83: William K. Sacco. 84: John H. Ostrom. 85: Tom Bean/DRK Photo. 86: (left and right) David Cupp. 86-87: Brian Milne/P.G. 87: David Cupp. 88: (left) National Park Service/U.S. Department of the Interior; (right) Chip Clark. 89: Chip Clark. 90-91: Chip Clark. 92-93: Everett C. Johnson/PHOTRI.

**Library of Congress Cataloging in Publication Data**

Main entry under title:

Ranger Rick's dinosaur book.

Includes index.
Summary: Text and illustrations present the physical characteristics, habits, and changing natural environment of the various kinds of dinosaurs that roamed the earth more than sixty-five million years ago.
1. Dinosaurs—Juvenile literature. [1. Dinosaurs] I. National Wildlife Federation. II. Title: Dinosaur Book.

QE862.D5R29 1984    567.9'1    8414680
ISBN 0-912186-54-2

## Acknowledgments

One fascinating aspect of dinosaurs is the fact that they are no longer around. It is exciting for us to imagine what they looked like and how they behaved. Yet we must remember how the scientists interpret the fossil record. For that interpretation, we relied on our scientific consultant, Dr. John Ostrom, one of the country's leading paleontologists. Dr. Ostrom reviewed all of our early text drafts as well as the sketches for our newly commissioned art.

Further assistance on some individual creatures was provided by Dr. Wann Langston, Professor of Geology, University of Texas, and Director of the Vertebrate Paleontology Laboratory, Texas Memorial Museum; and by Raymond Rye, Museum Specialist, Smithsonian Institution. Their cooperation made our work significantly easier.

## National Wildlife Federation

Dr. Jay D. Hair
*Executive Vice President*

James D. Davis
*Senior Vice President, Membership Development and Publications*

## Staff for this Book

Howard F. Robinson
*Managing Editor*

Victor H. Waldrop
*Project Editor and Writer*

Michael E. Loomis
*Art Editor and Writer*

Donna Miller
*Design Director*

Jeanne Turner
*Designer*

Dr. John H. Ostrom, Curator of Vertebrate Paleontology, Peabody Museum of Natural History, and Professor of Geology and Geophysics, Yale University
*Scientific Consultant*

Donna J. Reynolds
*Editorial Assistant*

Margaret E. Wolf
*Permissions Editor*

Priscilla Sharpless
*Production Manager*

Pam McCoy
*Production Artist*

NATIONAL WILDLIFE FEDERATION
1412 Sixteenth Street, N.W., Washington, D.C. 20036